To Dad,
with love from
1973.

GLENELG

1836 — 1972

first edition : 1,000 copies

published March 1973 by T. J. Strehlow
printing : Specialty Printers Adelaide
cover design : Don Gare
cover photography : Bill Neve
registered in Australia
for transmission by post as a book
National Library of Australia
card number & ISBN 0959949011

TABLE OF CONTENTS

FOREWORD 8

INTRODUCTION 9

CHAPTER ONE 11
The Years Before Foundation: Little Paradise

CHAPTER TWO 20
The Search For Identity: Glenelg as a Port or Fort

CHAPTER THREE 29
The Growth and Function of Nineteenth Century Glenelg: The Resort

CHAPTER FOUR 49
Community Life in Victorian Glenelg

CHAPTER FIVE 62
Twentieth Century Glenelg: The Urban Encroachment

BIBLIOGRAPHY 92

REFERENCES 94

INDEX OF PERSONAL NAMES AND SHIPS 99

disturbed the settlers' sleep "shouting their war whoops while dancing around their fires,"[10] but they proved surprisingly friendly, especially when the settlers appealed to their partiality for biscuits.[11]

For 12 months the settlers lived under terrible conditions in tents and slab huts, while those in command haggled over the site for the capital. The flies and heat of summer could not be escaped in tents, and an eye inflamation (ophthalmia) caused great discomfort. None of the settlers could permanently establish their homes or properties because this settlement was only temporary. Twenty-eight years later, Mary Thomas wrote: "all the gold of the Victorian mines would not induce me to undergo (the year in tents) again."[12]

Glenelg 1836 — one of the few pre-fabricated wooden huts

(S.A. Archives)

Despite the hardships suffered and the complaints over delays in establishing the capital, the settlers had only praise for the plains. Glenelg was then a verdant and lightly wooded plain, laced with fresh water lagoons leading down to a broad and firm beach. Many of the middle and upper class settlers saw Glenelg through the eyes of a gamekeeper. Passages like the following repeatedly appear in their letters:

> Game is in great abundance on the plain; it is almost impossible to walk two hundred yards without putting up quails; wild ducks and water-fowl are to be met with constantly on the river and in the lagoons.[13]

When the settlers left Holdfast Bay and Glenelg for their new, permanent homes in Adelaide in 1838, they took with them a love of the countryside and beach that was to draw well over 1,000 bidders back to Glenelg when a town was planned there in 1839.

The first landing place — "Little Paradise"
(From a sketch by Col. Light, S.A. Archives)

The physical features of Glenelg (see map B) suggested to Col. Light a site for a town and even its possible function, before he found the Port River.

> Looking generally at this place I am quite confident it will be one of the largest settlements if not the capital of the new colony. The creek will be its harbour. Six months labour would clear a road down to it, and if not, there is a hard sandy beach the whole way on which a mail coach might run.[14]

The Port River was discovered soon after Light wrote this, and Adelaide was built to use this river as its port. However, although Glenelg was only a roadstead,[15] and its little river could never have provided the large harbour necessary for a capital city, for years it remained the safest anchorage on the coast for large ships. It was not until the end of the nineteenth century that Glenelg's position as a port was finally doomed by the building of Outer Harbour.

In 1838, Glenelg had been almost entirely deserted by the settlers, who had moved to Adelaide. Mr. J. B. Neales landed at Holdfast Bay as an immigrant in 1838, and "the first white man he saw was Mr. Findon, and the first house he entered was the Reed Hut."[16] The Reed Hut was a grog shanty, and Mr. Findon was its unlicenced proprietor. The constant arrival of immigrant ships maintained a small settlement of huts and tents, but until the new town was surveyed by Light in 1839, the grog shanty was the only permanent building at Glenelg.

This shanty was an improvement on previous arrangements. While the settlers had lived at Glenelg, marines had been stationed to guard the colony's rum supply on the beach. This arrangement was unsatisfactory, to say the least, for "the number of 'Dead Marines' in immediate proximity to the living told its own tale."[17] The shanty was not much improvement as Mr. Neales found when he ordered drinks for himself and two sailors: "the charge was a staggerer, gin and water 4d, porter for the two men, 5/6."[18]

The city of Adelaide was still no more than a collection of tents and prefabricated wooden houses brought out from England. The colony had no roads, and Glenelg was connected to Adelaide by "a well defined track made by the wheels of a bullock dray."[19] The Sturt River had to be crossed without a bridge, and the muddy track to Adelaide grew increasingly worse as more people used it.

CHAPTER TWO

THE SEARCH FOR IDENTITY: GLENELG AS A PORT OR FORT

GLENELG was meant to be a port. The new colony of South Australia was isolated on all sides by unexplored land and a vast ocean. With no food produced within the colony for the first years, it relied entirely upon the life-line of sea travel. For five months the colony had no official port and violent controversy raged over Col. Light's choice of the Port River. When Glenelg was opened in 1839, it was hailed as the colony's potentially best and perhaps only large port. Glenelg's violently fluctuating fortunes as a port and its short lived attempt to build a fortress were major parts in its long search for a permanent identity.

The 65 acres reserved for Glenelg were opened for sale early in 1839 (see map C). As 1400 tenders were received and the land was to be sold at a fixed price of one pound per acre, the Governor decided to pick the purchaser through a lottery. William Finke's syndicate including Osmond Gilles and H. R. Wigley was drawn, and they bought what was to be the whole of Glenelg for £65. The job of surveying and subdividing Glenelg was given to Light Finnis and Co. Although Col. Light was then near death, the plan, which was published in October 1839, bears his stamp in its carefully planned grid and in the multiple names for single streets. (The names were not given with the original plan, as shown in map C). Governor Gawler had expressed a wish that Glenelg should be developed as a port,[1] and Light's plan certainly supports this. Along the side of the muddy creek which he named Thames (this was soon changed to its more appropriate name, Patawalonga) is indicated a "Custom House Quay", a "Government Reserve" ("G.R." in the plan) is placed near it with the building of a Harbour Master's residence in mind. High hopes were universally expressed on the effect of building the jetty, which Light also planned for the near future.

> It is quite certain if the jetty proposed by Col. Light is constructed, that Glenelg will become the sole landing place for cattle and sheep, as well as for cargoes of ships whose tonnage prevents their entering Port Adelaide.[2]

Despite the financial squeeze of the previous decade, public confidence in Glenelg was very high. Even before the Governor had approved the plan, a newspaper article called capitalists' attention to Glenelg, "as affording a safe investment and an immediate lucrative return."[3] In May 1839, a customs house was being built on the Government reserve, and by June, a large-scale building company, the

MAP C

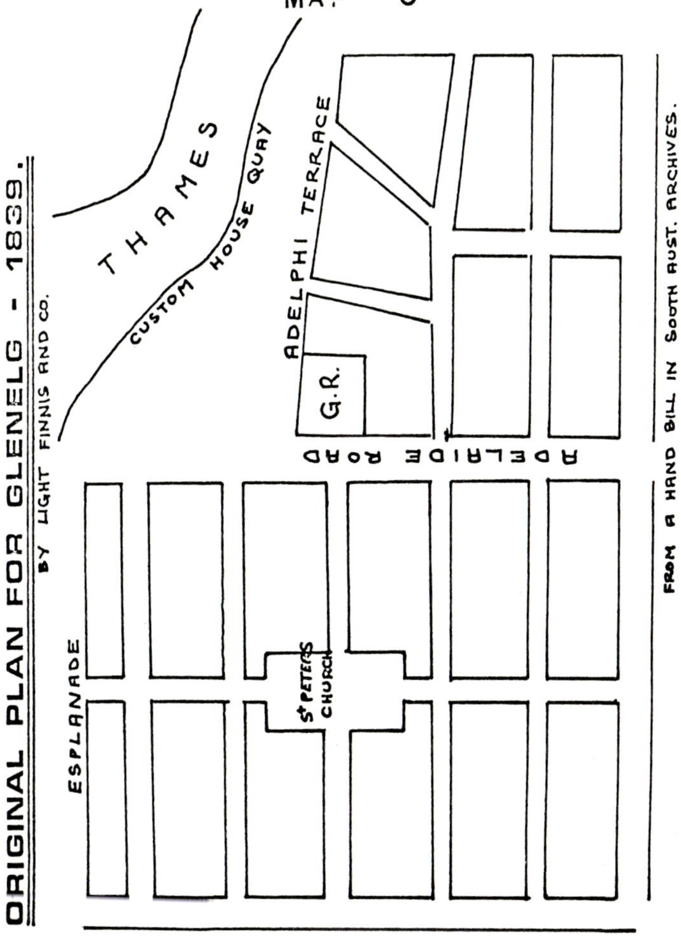

Glenelg Crescent Development Company had been formed, with capital of £20,000 in £10 shares, to construct a large crescent of buildings fronting the sea for rental to the colonists.[4] The intention was to develop the area as a resort, but apparently it was before its time. Little is reported of the company's fate, but no crescent was built. In that same month however, 27 allotments "in the best parts of the town"[5] were offered for sale by auction. By November, a second large-scale public development company, the Pier and Warehouse Company, was formed, with capital of £2,000 in £10 shares.[6] This time the plan was to develop Glenelg specifically as a port.

Glenelg now had the beginnings of a jetty. During the ceremonial driving of the first pile, Governor Gawler said "the existing landing places are a disgrace of horses along the way, only to find that he had been beaten. A *Register* man had rowed out to meet the steamer in the gulf before it had been sighted at Glenelg.[18]

Captain Duff was appointed Harbour Master in 1859, but it was not until 1865 that the first merchant vessel discharged its cargo at the jetty. Pacific and Oriental steamers called at the jetty with mail and passengers until 1873, when everything changed suddenly.

Steam cranes and railway tracks on the Glenelg Jetty in the 1880s
(S.A. Archives)

In August 1873, the first railway from Adelaide to Glenelg was opened. The journey to the city was cut to 30 minutes, and for the first time in Glenelg's history large scale shipment of cargo was possible. The Adelaide, Glenelg and Suburban Railway Company initially used four goods trucks and a single track which allowed trains all the way up to the jetty. However, all return journeys had to be made in reverse, for the railway as yet had no loop lines. Within a year, the company had doubled its number of goods trucks. By 1880, a second and more extensive railway had been opened, though it amalgamated with the first within a year. The Glenelg Railway Company was, by the 1880s, well established. The jetty was equipped with steam cranes, and lines ran along its full length. Business boomed, and Glenelg at last could boast of being a large port.

John Lee was the secretary of the Glenelg Institute and was very well known for his work in developing the place. In 1883, he wrote a proud booklet on Glenelg called "Historic Guide", largely to attract visitors and to promote Glenelg as a seaside resort. Although it revealed much about Glenelg as a port, the booklet shows that the new role, of a resort, was challenging Glenelg's function as a port almost as soon as it had become one.

The jetty had a lighthouse placed at the sea end, and a hulk was moored off shore to indicate the P & O anchorage and to hold its coal supplies. A special train was always waiting to take mail and passengers swiftly into Adelaide, while cargo was loaded onto trucks and pulled behind the passenger trains. John Lee claimed that once 460 tons of cargo had been delivered to Adelaide within 36 hours of arriving at the jetty.[19] In 1883, the railway owned eight acres of goods yards in Glenelg, and Lee boasted that its forges could turn out perfect screws over 10 feet long.[20] In the five years before his book was written, Lee quotes the value of imports as rising some 300%, to nearly half a million pounds sterling.[21] The railway carried 50% more passengers in the same period, which amounted to well over a million people in the year 1883. Glenelg's function as a seaside resort was obviously booming as well and to some extent at the expense of its function as a port. The foreshore began to mushroom with tents and roundabouts, rather than steam cranes and warehouses. The tourists were proving more profitable than the cargoes which passed through Glenelg.

Port Adelaide in this period was making considerable headway towards establishing itself as Adelaide's port. The town had been raised above flood level with the silt dredged from the Port River, and the Harbour could now take ships of considerable size. The town had expanded over the whole river area and was in too strong a position for Glenelg to challenge by 1900.

Several blows sealed Glenelg's fate as a port. In 1886, the Chamier Harbour Scheme was planned and executed with too little professional help. In a freak flood and storm the expensive works were completely destroyed. Altogether six attempts were made to construct boat harbours at Glenelg, and each one ended in disaster. The Chamier Scheme left the Council in debt for a quarter of a century, and the later schemes proved only more expensive and just as unsuccessful. The fifth attempt, in 1916, left the Government with a debt of £42,232. By this time there was little intent to form a harbour for commercial purposes, for the plans called for a promenade three-quarters of a mile long ending with a magnificent amusement pavilion. When in 1958 the Patawalonga was at last successfully built into a boat harbour, a commercial port was far from the developers' minds.

One detour in the search remains to be examined. During the 1880s, Glenelg came close to being a fortified town. Early in February 1882, the residents of Glenelg awoke one morning to find three warships anchored in Holdfast Bay. Not even the Government had known of the visit before that morning. Their shock at discovering that these were Russian warships was exceeded only by the hospitality with which they welcomed them. Admiral Aslanbegoff was on a goodwill visit, and he and his men were given outings, dinner and a Grand Ball, which Governor Jervois attended. Amongst the visiting crew was a sailor named Rimsky-Korsakoff who later became a famous composer. However, as soon as the Russians had left, it occurred to the worthy citizens of Glenelg that the incident had shown the colony's unpreparedness in the case of an attack. In March 1885, Glenelg's Mayor pointed out that £200,000 worth of buildings on the seafront were totally unprotected. Glenelg's Council asked that the ship *Protector* be positioned closer to Glenelg, in case a Russian cruiser paid another visit. Apparently the same hospitality was not to be shown a second time. On April 17, 1885, in a public meeting at the Glenelg Town Hall, the Government announced that it was about to build a large fort one and a half miles north of the Patawalonga. On April 20 the Mayor attempted to enrol volunteers. An entire railway and a new road (now Military Road) were built to the site of the new fort, and in June 1888, two huge guns and one hundred tons of fittings arrived from England. The guns were of the latest design, were 25 feet long, and weighed 20 tons each.[22]

In May a difficulty in purchasing the land stopped work. A Bill was introduced into Parliament to give the Government the power to buy land at a fair price, but although it was passed, nothing more was heard of the fort. The road remains, but the railway was dismantled only a month after it was laid. The fort was not even started. Months after the Parliamentary Bill had been passed, an anxious Glenelg Council was given the reason for not building the fort: a military report had pointed out that if it had been built, Glenelg could be considered a fortified town, and "it would be quite within the ethics of warfare for Glenelg to be shelled."[23] No doubt, greatly comforted, the Council said no more, and more than 30 years later it was reported that the guns still lay abandoned in the sandhills of Glenelg.[24]

By the 1900s Glenelg had found its permanent identity as a seaside resort. It had been no more appropriate as a bastian of defence than as a port. Its broad beaches and country air were proving eminently more suited to a resort.

CHAPTER THREE

THE GROWTH AND FUNCTION OF NINETEENTH CENTURY GLENELG: THE RESORT

As a seaside resort, Glenelg was very successful. In the 1840s and 1850s, it was a marine retreat for the wealthy businessmen of Adelaide and their families, but railways and good roads brought a tremendous rise in popularity during the 1870s, and its whole character changed. This chapter examines the role played by Glenelg in the growth of nineteenth century Adelaide, and the changing face of Glenelg itself.

1836 - 1860

The first 40 years of Adelaide's growth show a radial pattern of development (see Adelaide Urban Area Map 1876, page 36). The central city area laid out by Col. Light was the main administrative, commercial and business centre. Along the rivers and main roads, small villages grew to assume functions which were to characterize them later as suburbs. North Adelaide was a residential district, while areas close to the city, such as Norwood and Hindmarsh, grew as working class districts and later as industrial areas. Small isolated villages such as Marion and Plympton became focal points for development, as more people built homes away from the city amongst the farms and orchards of the Adelaide Plains. Thus, Adelaide grew outwards from a number of centres which were distributed radially around the city on main roads and water courses.[1] Glenelg was amongst these earliest and largest of the radial developments. There were less tangible reasons for its growth than can be seen in the growth of other villages and new suburbs. Its only assets were "cool sands and sparkling waters,"[2] but by the 1850s, these had proved themselves quite adequate.

Two reporters, assigned to walk to Glenelg from Adelaide city[3] in 1851, recorded the lack of urban development between the two centres. They only occasionally came upon small villages, such as Netley and Cowandilla, for the majority of their walk took them through open fields, "everywhere oats grown for hay or under the scythe for meadow hay." Towards Glenelg, they noted vineyards and orchards, with "cattle in all directions" in the fields. The village of Plympton was typical of the small settlements they encountered along the way. It consisted of 10 houses and a small Wesleyan Chapel. Thus, they were impressed by the size of Glenelg when they arrived there, for it contained 80 houses and over 250 people.[4] They described the houses they saw as "substantial large brick edifaces" or "marine villas", although they also saw cottages and huts associated

A private house typical of Glenelg's earliest villas, in the area of the original town of 1839

(Author's photograph)

with the ships that called there. They described Glenelg as an upper class marine retreat and mentioned some of the well-known Adelaide dignitaries who lived there. Dr. Yates, a member of the Legislative Council, lived just out of town, and the Stipendiary Magistrate of the Adelaide Local Court had a large house in Glenelg, which they wished had been "more in taste with our notions of a marine villa."[5]

Glenelg was an island of upper class residential development far from the business and commercial centre of the city, and thus, performed a unique function in the development of Adelaide. Although only the wealthy could afford to live in Glenelg, where there was little or no employment, and work in the city every day, anyone could catch an omnibus or coach to Glenelg at weekends for a holiday. Public transport was in the erratic hands of private enterprise and was too expensive and unreliable to be used for daily transport. The "spring cart", run daily from Adelaide to Glenelg by Thomas Haymes, cost 2/6 return, but the five passengers were as likely to arrive on foot as in the cart on account of the swampy road. Mr. McDonald imported three large omnibuses from Glasgow, called them 'The Rose", "The Shamrock" and "The Thistle", and painted each in different Scottish tartans for the run. Richard George, known as "Flash Dick", also made the run. However, it was not until Cobb and Co. bought them out, and the railway was established that cheap dependable travel could allow commuting between Glenelg and Adelaide.

The poor communications with Adelaide therefore ensured that only the wealthy with their own transport could afford to live in Glenelg. However, transport was sufficient to allow large crowds to gather at Glenelg on holidays.

The old Governor's residence was a drive-in bottle department for St. Leonard's Inn in 1969, but was demolished in 1970

(Author's photograph)

A ceiling in the Governor's residence

(Author's photograph)

This became the second most important function of Glenelg in the 1850s. It was the only settlement along the coast and was often the centre of make-do colonial sports, such as the Beach Race Meeting in 1855. The meeting attracted many men of "neat cord and comely boot top"[6] and must have been one of the few races in Adelaide's history to have been cut short by rising tides.

Photograph A1 taken from the Family Hotel (see Map A, Glenelg 1870)
(S.A. Archives)

The buildings at Glenelg illustrated both its popularity as a resort and the upper class atmosphere of the town. The Glenelg Hotel had been operating for 10 years, and had been joined in the 1850s by St. Leonards Inn and the Berkshire and Pier Hotels. They were all large structures, most being two stories and of elegant appearance. Unlike the inns and pubs of the city, these hotels were designed to accept paying visitors rather than to cater for a large bar-room business. Indicative of the high tone of Glenelg as a resort was the Governor's summer residence, built in the centre of the town facing the Patawalonga. There were already three large churches, built by the Methodists, Congregationalists, and Anglicans, the religions of the establishment in South Australia. Some of the houses built by private citizens reached monumental proportions, although most were elegant two storied family mansions.

1860 - 1870

The census of 1861 gives the first detailed statistical picture of Glenelg. From the mass of figures, a pattern emerges which fits in well with the picture of Glenelg already apparent in the 1840s and 1850s. The housing figures for Adelaide city and Glenelg (see Graph A) show that the majority of houses in the city had two, three or four rooms, as might be expected in a middle-class dominated society. However, at Glenelg the majority of houses were either very small, with two rooms, or very large, with over six rooms. The photograph (A1) taken in the mid 1860s shows how this pattern may be interpreted. (The map of the subdivided area of Glenelg of 1870 indicates this area to be undeveloped, but because widely separated mansions were probably not considered part of subdivisions, the area of Glenelg was much larger than shown). The large houses are the private mansions of the city businessmen and

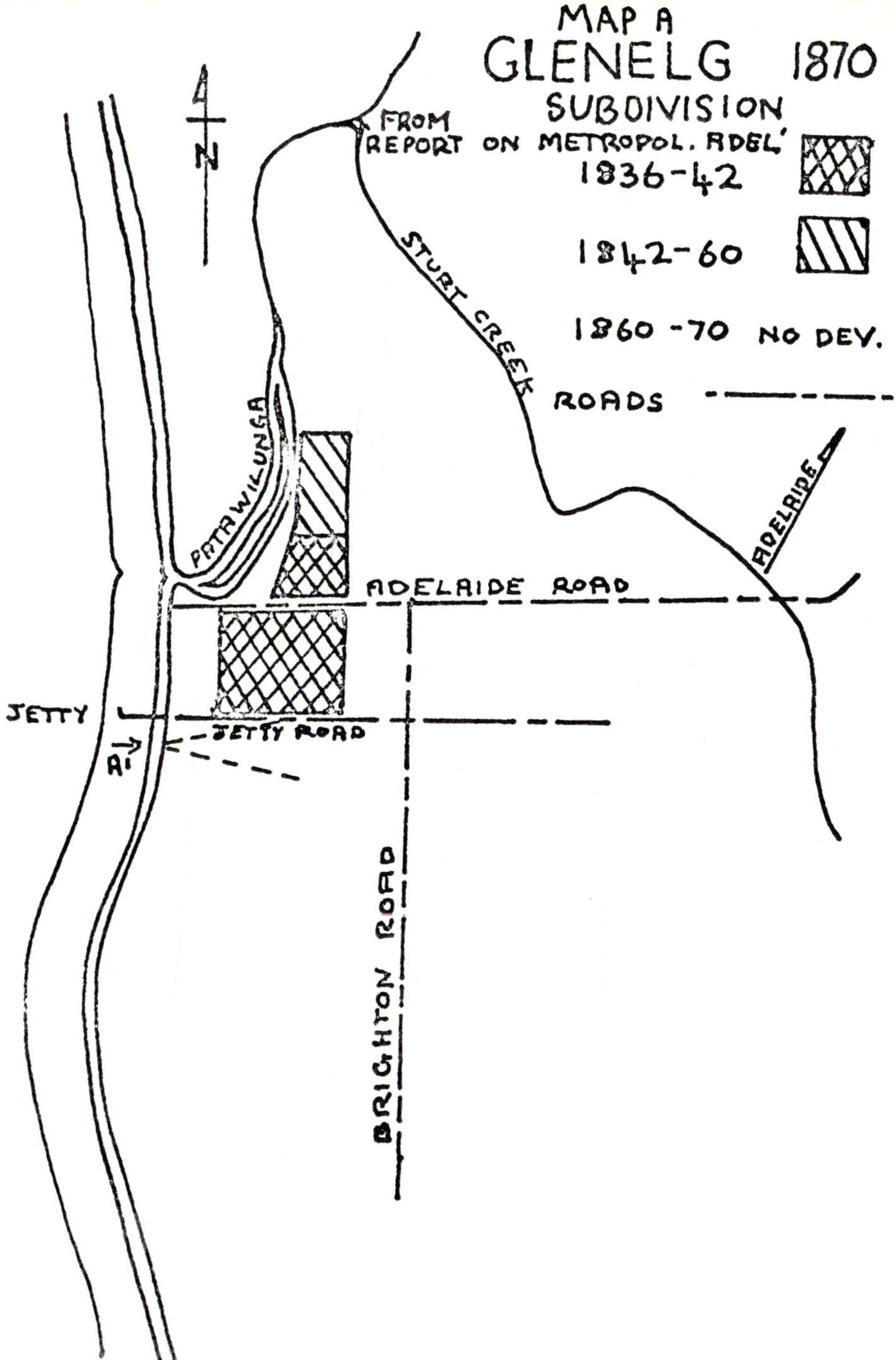

MAP A
GLENELG 1870
SUBDIVISION
FROM REPORT ON METROPOL. ADEL'
1836-42
1842-60
1860-70 NO DEV.
ROADS
N
STURT CREEK
PATAWILUNGA
ADELAIDE
ADELAIDE ROAD
JETTY
JETTY ROAD
A'
BRIGHTON ROAD

GRAPH A

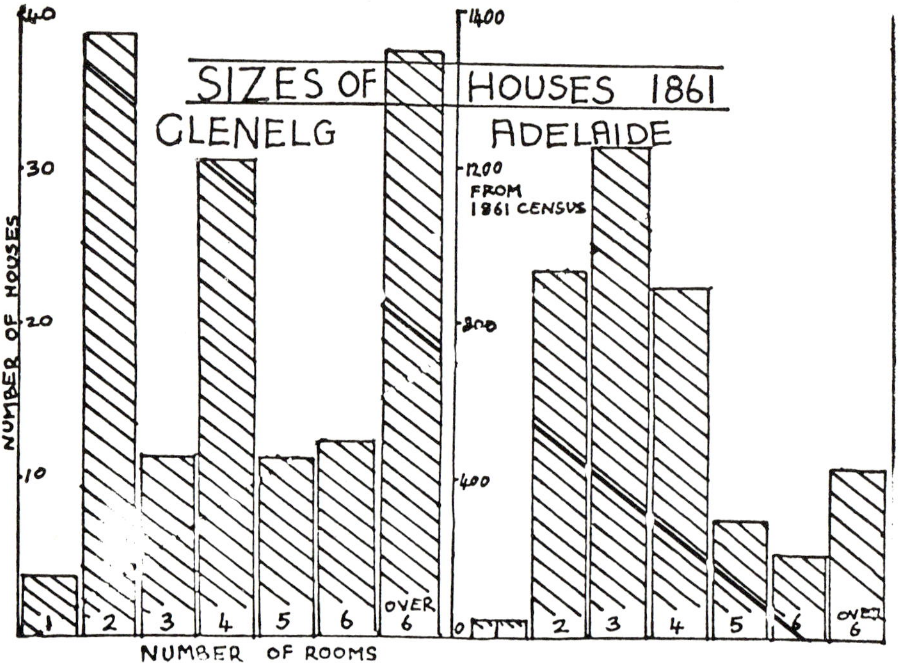

dignitaries. However, because of the small percentage of labourers and farmers at Glenelg, and the fact that one-fifth of all the females there were domestic servants,[7] the small houses must have been servants' quarters. Servants only required small quarters for sleeping in, and it is possible that many lived in the mansions. In 1970, this pattern of housing is still apparent in the oldest parts of Glenelg. The mansions, now subdivided as flats, are surrounded by a cluster of very small old houses. Another facet of this pattern is indicated by the large proportion of houses at Glenelg classified as "uninhabited".[8] The proportion is almost twice that of Adelaide and can be explained by the resort nature of Glenelg. Many houses were left unattended for parts of the year when the family lived in the city.

A similar pattern emerges also from the population figures. There is a slight predominance of females in Adelaide, as would be expected of a town, but in Glenelg, the 421 females vastly outnumbered the 287 males.[9] The greater proportion of females in Glenelg could be attributed to the predominance of mansions and servants' quarters seen in the housing pattern. In the city of Adelaide nearly half of all working women were employed in jobs other than that of servants. In Glenelg the number of women domestic servants was seven times the number of women employed in other pursuits.[10] The occupations of the male population at Glenelg showed that only 48.8% worked for a living, while in Adelaide the percentage working was 56.1%. The larger number of dependent males at Glenelg is typical of a residential community, and the percentage of children, relatives and visitors also indicates this. However, it must be remembered that Glenelg at this time was a much smaller community than the city of Adelaide, having a population about one twenty-fifth the size of the city population.[11]

By 1871, Adelaide's population had increased by 54% over the previous decade. In the same period, Glenelg's had increased by 87% and had changed in character. New roads and the arrival of Cobb and Co. coaches between Adelaide and Glenelg started to effect Glenelg's popularity. The census of 1871 showed that in Glenelg, the proportion of female servants had dropped from 21.1% of the female population in 1861 to 19% in 1871. Even more significantly, the proportion of women in other jobs or trades had risen. The proportion of dependent women at Glenelg was below that of Adelaide city in 1871,[12] and the proportion of dependent males also fell. Increases in the population came mainly from larger numbers of children, relatives, and visitors. Thus, Glenelg was becoming less of an upper class residential area as its population climbed. More people visited Glenelg, and more people stayed to build their homes there, as employment opportunities rose and it became easier to commute to the city. The changes becoming evident during the 1860s were to accelerate during the following decade.

THE 1870s AND 1880s

Adelaide in the early 1870s still showed the radial development characteristic of the previous 30 years. The isolated areas of development had yet to join, and Glenelg remained a very separate community surrounded by farms and orchards. Yet during the decade of the 1870s Glenelg's population increased by 105.7%, while Adelaide's population showed only a 41.4% increase. The development boom, that had begun in the sixties, was accelerating during the seventies as the whole of Adelaide experienced a building boom. By 1876 Glenelg had increased enormously in area under subdivision and in population (see Map B, Glenelg 1876 Subdivision, page 39).

One of the most important reasons for this boom was the opening in 1873 of the first railway from Adelaide to Glenelg. By 1880, a second company opened a line, which was soon amalgamated with the first. The difference that these railways made to Glenelg's popularity was enormous. Luxurious imported American first class carriages were run on the Glenelg lines, and even the second class carriages were ornate by today's standards. Carriages were designed to hold 50 to 60 passengers, but it became common for as many as 30 extra men to crowd onto the open platforms at either end of the carriages.[13] On race days at Morphettville, goods trucks were pressed into passenger service, and even then men rode on the roof. Trains left Adelaide for Glenelg 26 times a day during the week, from six in the morning until 11 at night. Return tickets were 1/6 first class and 1/- second class. Special tickets, for as little as 1/-, were issued on race days to cover both the journey to Morphettville Racecourse and the entrance fees. At weekends a standing concession reduced the second class return fare to 6d. "Special Excursion" tickets dropped the price again to only 3d. return. Thus, the trains enabled an enormous number of holiday makers to visit Glenelg, as well as allowing residents of Glenelg to commute to the city cheaply and efficiently. By the early 1880s the trains were carrying over one million passengers a year.

Although Glenelg was changing, its old character still dominated the town. The old pattern of isolated mansions, with their clusters of stables and servants' quarters, still dominated a photograph taken in the eighties (see photograph B1, page 37). Another photograph (see photograph B3, page 40), of the centre of the

ADELAIDE URBAN AREA.

1876

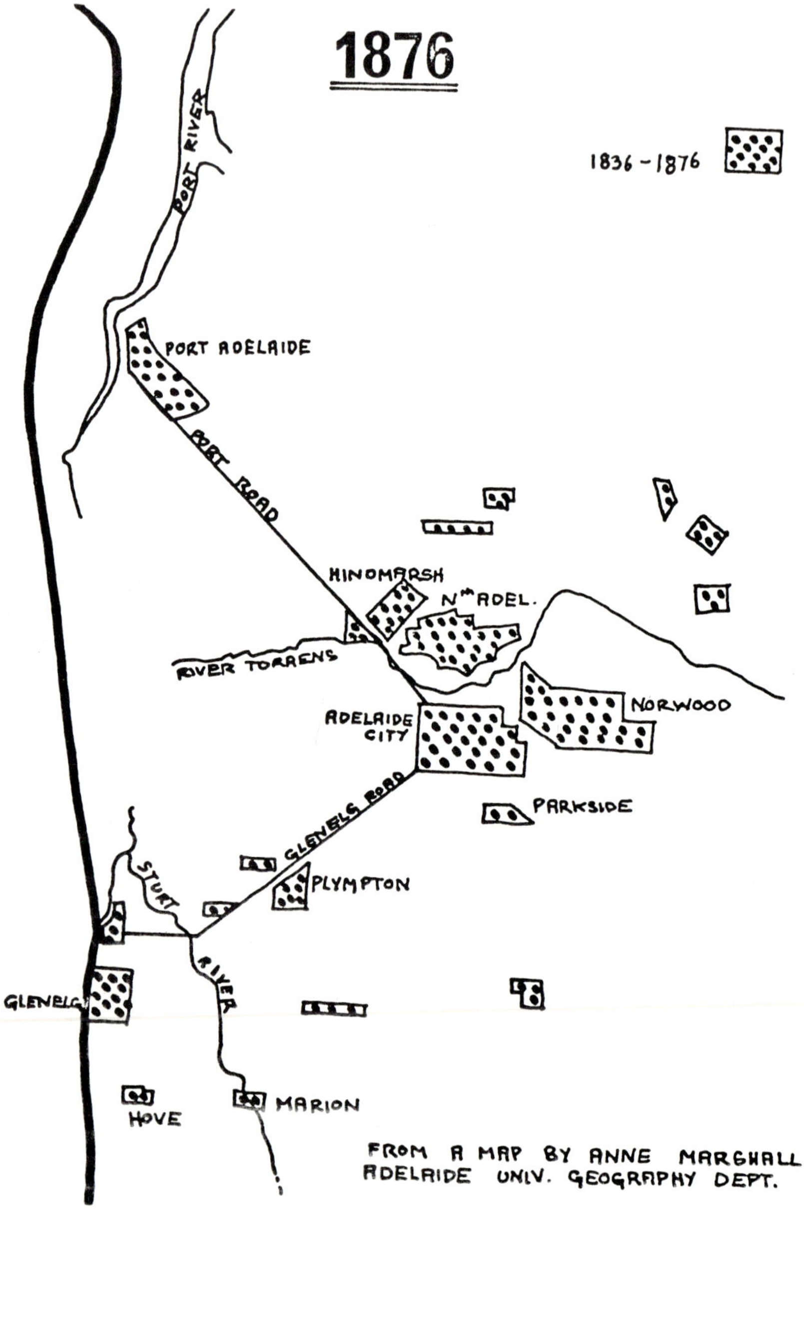

old town of Glenelg, still shows the characteristic pattern of mansions and cottages, but the increased population caused a greater density of housing. Small business establishments and middle sized houses of the growing proportion of working and commercial class residents were filling in the spaces between the older mansions. Glenelg as a town and community was growing in size and complexity.

Photograph B1, Outer Glenelg, taken between 1872-86

(S.A. Archives)

During the seventies, four impressively large, new hotels were built. The Terminus Hotel, at the head of the railway, was only a minute's walk away from the grand Pier Hotel. The smaller Family Hotel was built on the foreshore to cater for holidaymakers, while the Globe and Broadway Hotels were built amongst the recently developed areas to the south of old Glenelg. In the same period only one church was built, the Church of Christ. The seventies also saw the development of many features which would attract permanent residents. In 1875, both mains pressure water and gas were connected. In the same year the Glenelg State School was opened, and the magnificent Glenelg Institute was built at the foot of the jetty. A fire brigade, though rudimentary, was established in 1877. The possibilities for entertainments within the town also increased. The jetty was extended, and in 1878, a skating rink, costing over £1,500, was opened in the centre of Glenelg. At its opening, effective use was made of the new gas supply, for 31 gas lamps were placed around the rink. However, the venture did not last long, but it failed only because of poor planning. By 1880 Glenelg had become so popular that a railway was built south along the beach from

Photograph B2, The Old Gum Tree, 1870 (see Map B, page 39)
(S.A. Archives)

Glenelg to Marino Rocks. As a port Glenelg was also enjoying great popularity, for the railway doubled its rolling stock within two years of its establishment.

The rest of Adelaide did not experience Glenelg's boom. The great building boom that caused the mushrooming growth of Adelaide (shown in the 1886 Urban Development Map, page 42) did not occur until after Glenelg's sudden boom in popularity in the seventies. This can, in part, be explained by Glenelg's isolation from the city, for the train trip was often described as "the prettiest trip in Adelaide".[14] The trip even had its romance, for the "leafy woods . . . (which) remind one of the woodlands at home"[15] were none other than the "remnants of the Black Forest once notorious as the hiding place of cattle stealers and other desperados."[16] The Glenelg and Marino railway was also very attractive, although

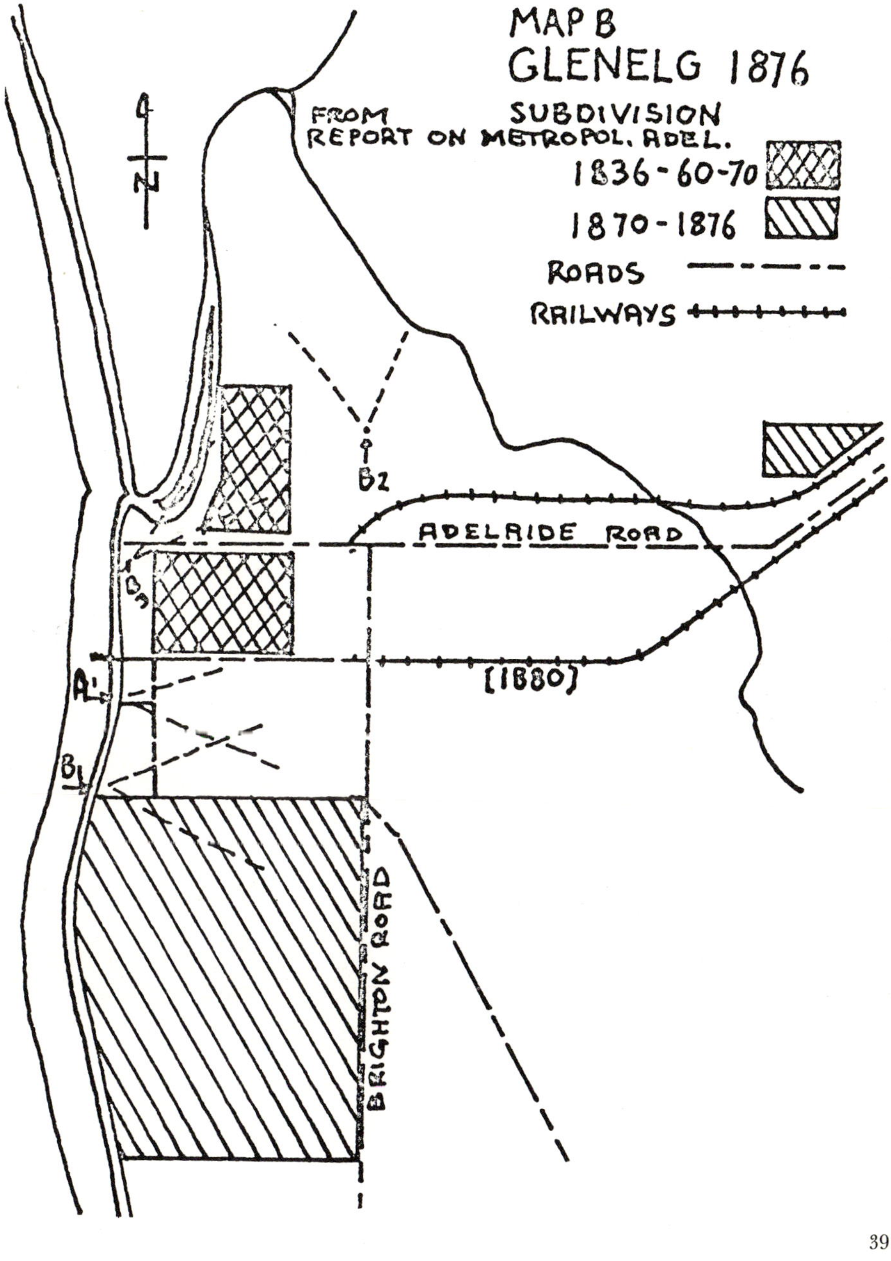

it must have been unnerving when drivers who were "used to sand"[17] happily drove over rails covered by several inches of it. A photograph of the Old Gum Tree[18] in 1870 also illustrates how close the countryside was to Glenelg (see Photograph B2).

By the end of the 1870s, Adelaide too was experiencing a building and population boom. By 1880, the population of the Adelaide area had more than doubled, from 43,000 to 100,000. In 1886, Adelaide's urban area had increased enormously (see Urban Area Map 1886, p. 42) and the area under subdivision in Glenelg had also greatly increased. The population growth rate for the country areas of South Australia had fallen for the first time in the State's history, and the country was entering a disastrous phase of setbacks and droughts. The city was becoming the dominating influence in all South Australia, and Glenelg's popularity rose correspondingly. The central business area as well as the residential areas expanded, and the changes which had been evident in the sixties and seventies became dominant.

A photograph from above the Family Hotel shows the gradual development of new areas of urban subdivision (see photograph C1). The large mansions were still evident, but many more smaller houses were being built. In the older areas, the big gardens of the mansions were being subdivided, and the smaller houses were required for the increasing proportion of middle class families at Glenelg. Small unmarked lanes (see photograph C2) wound between the mansions, warehouses, stables and cottages. The old economic and social patterns, established when Glenelg was still a marine retreat, were changing. The proportion of dependent males had dropped while the proportion of males in commerce or trade had risen. The percentage of male domestic servants had fallen from 3.5% in 1861 to practically nothing in 1881. Likewise the proportion of female domestic servants had fallen but the proportion of females teaching or in commerce had risen from one seventh of the working females in 1861 to nearly one quarter in 1881. Children, relatives, and visitors at Glenelg continued to rise in numbers to over 50% of all females in 1881.

Photograph B3, the centre of Glenelg in 1873 (see Map B)

(S.A. Archives)

MAP D

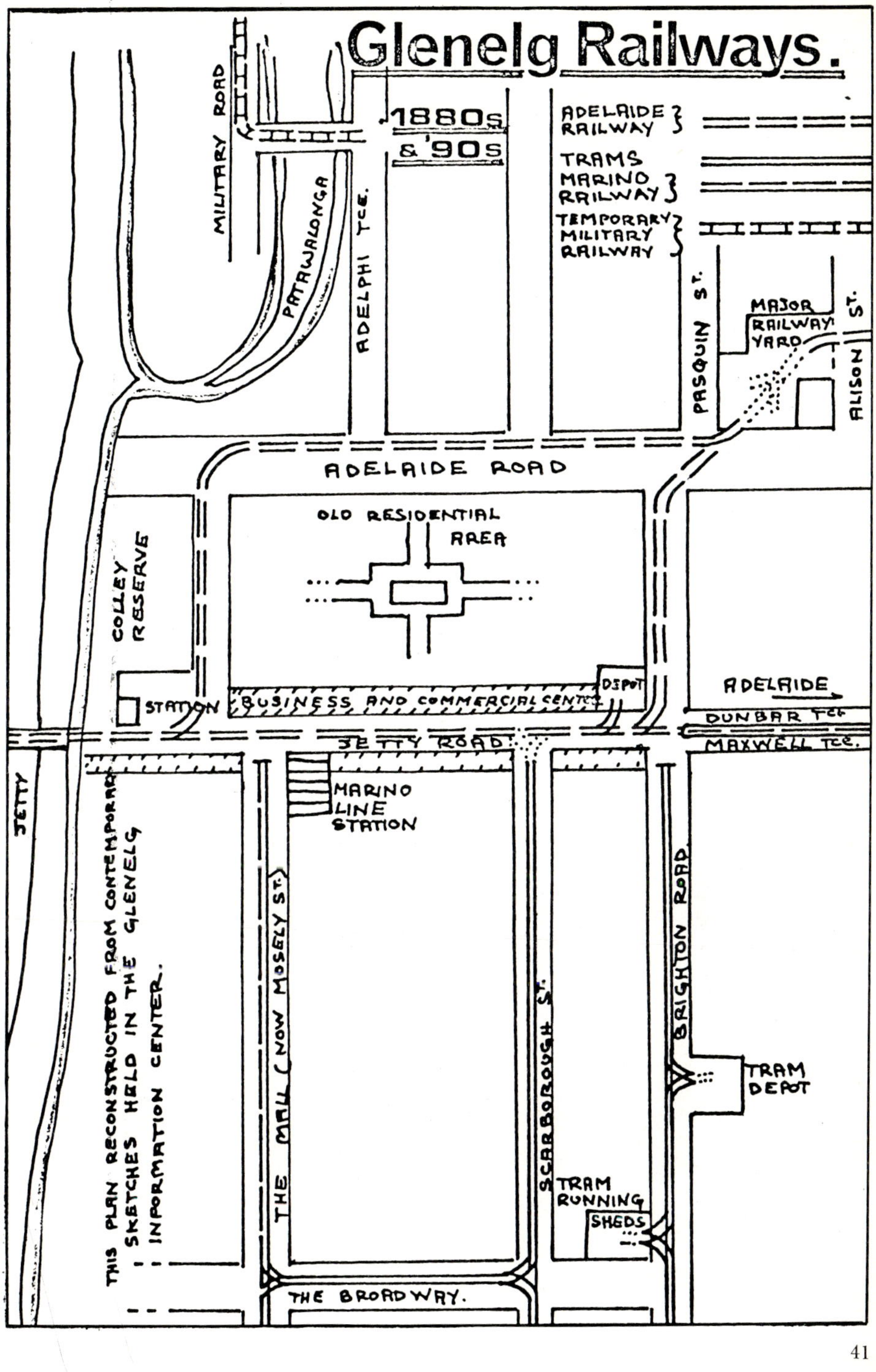
Glenelg Railways.
1880s & '90s
ADELAIDE RAILWAY
TRAMS
MARINO RAILWAY
TEMPORARY MILITARY RAILWAY
MILITARY ROAD
PATAWALONGA
ADELPHI TCE.
PASQUIN ST.
MAJOR RAILWAY YARD
ALISON ST.
ADELAIDE ROAD
OLD RESIDENTIAL AREA
COLLEY RESERVE
STATION
BUSINESS AND COMMERCIAL CENTRE
DEPOT
ADELAIDE
DUNBAR TCE
JETTY ROAD
MAXWELL TCE.
JETTY
MARINO LINE STATION
THIS PLAN RECONSTRUCTED FROM CONTEMPORARY SKETCHES HELD IN THE GLENELG INFORMATION CENTER.
THE MALL (NOW MOSELY ST.
SCARBOROUGH ST.
BRIGHTON ROAD
TRAM DEPOT
TRAM RUNNING SHEDS
THE BROADWAY.

ADELAIDE URBAN AREA.

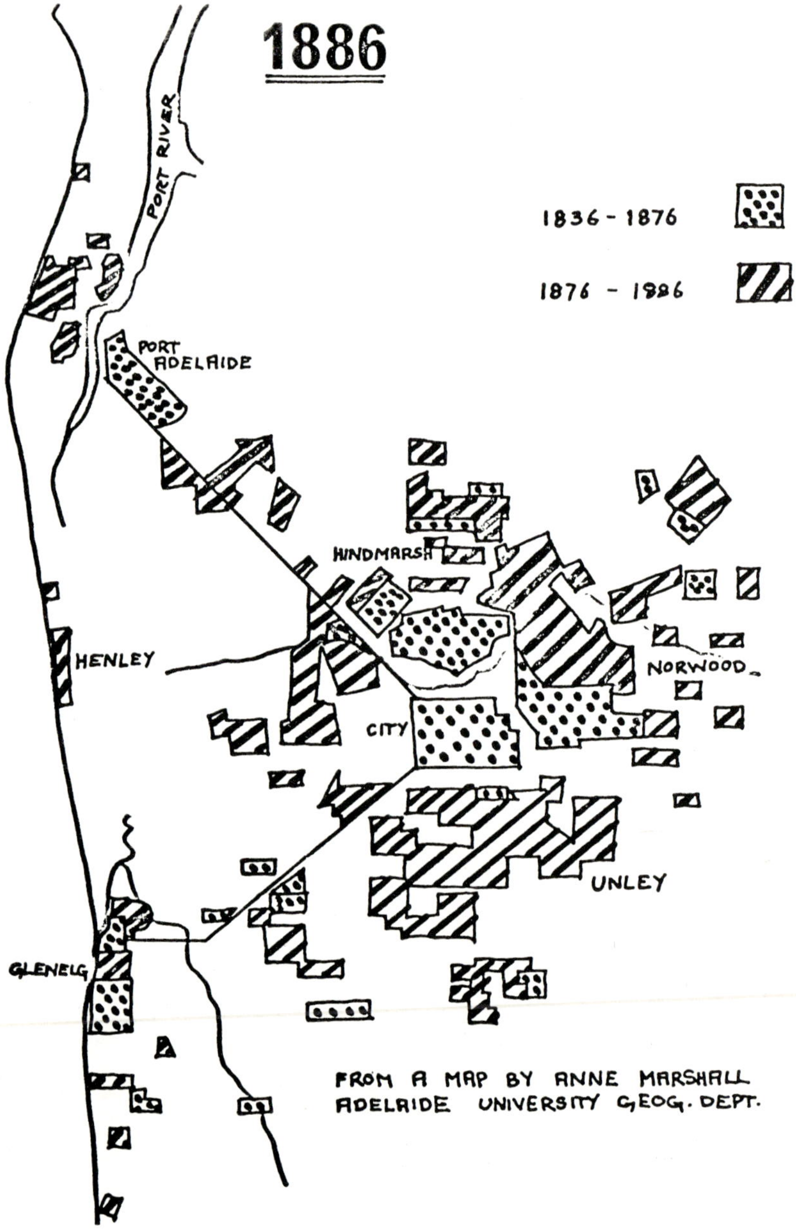

Photograph C1, the Family Hotel and open ground in what is now the centre of Glenelg (see Map C)

(S.A. Archives)

The change can most clearly be seen in the figures on housing in Glenelg and Adelaide. Unlike Glenelg in 1861, it now shows a distinct majority of houses in the three, four, and five room bracket. Although a higher proportion of houses in Glenelg had more rooms than the houses in Adelaide, the pattern of mansions and servants' quarters is gone. This is also indicated in the fall

Photograph C2, small unnamed lanes between the mansions remain little changed today

(Author's photograph)

in the ratio of relative population to houses. In 1861, Glenelg had a higher ratio (an average of 4½ people per house) than any other town in the Adelaide area. By 1881, it had the same ratio as Brighton, Kensington-Norwood, and Port Adelaide. The number of houses at Glenelg had not kept up with the population rise of the seventies,[20] but by 1881, a building boom was evident.

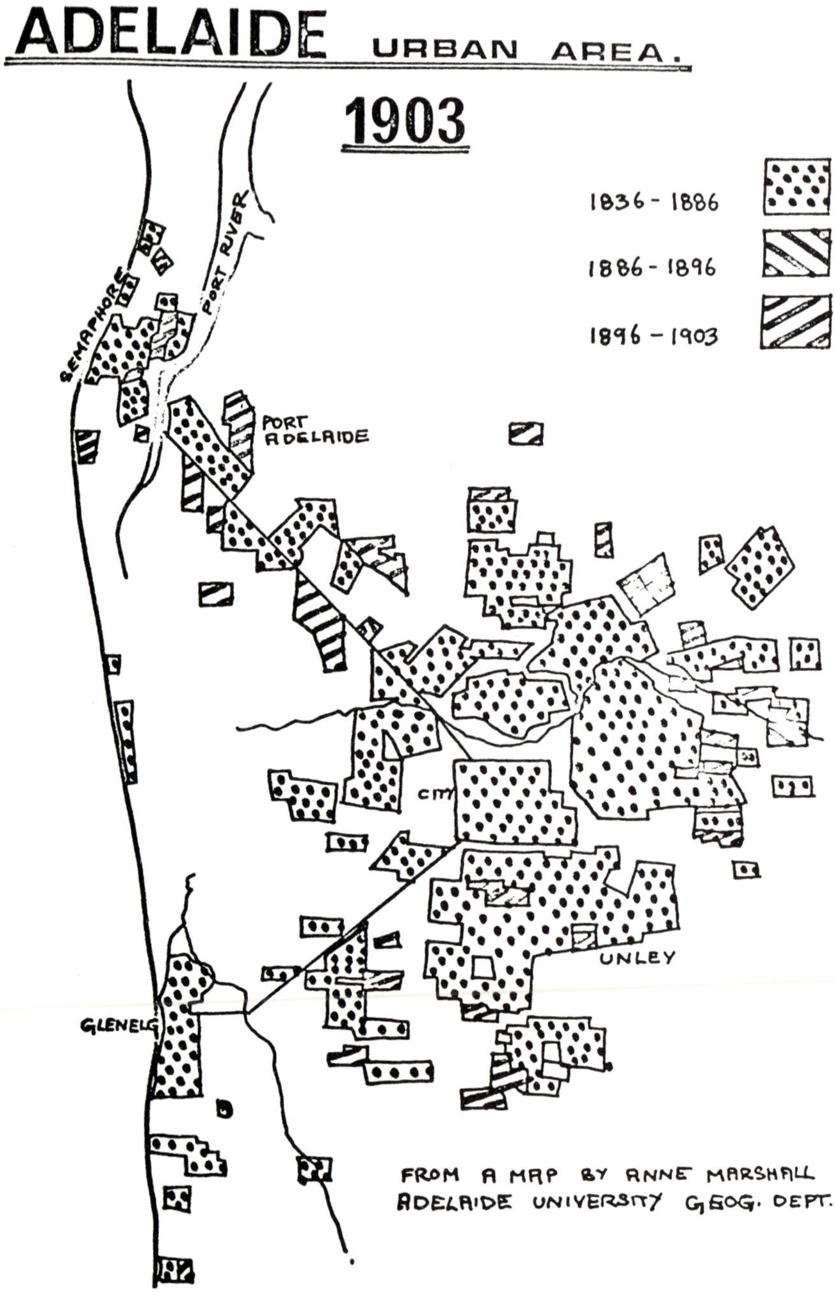

The assessment of land values shows an erratic growth, but a trend towards less expensive houses and properties seems evident.

The dramatic increase in Glenelg's popularity as a place to live in and to visit remained the major cause of these changes. During the seventies the number of passengers carried by trains to Glenelg rose rapidly and in the 1880s this rate was still increasing. The attractions of Glenelg increased with the years also, and its reputation as a place for a marvellous "day out" became far more famous than its old reputation as a select marine retreat.

The beach and esplanade, from the Town Hall, 29th December, 1913
(S.A. Archives)

In a world where instant pressure pack stimulation had yet to arrive, the fun came from "greasy poles, swimming and diving matches, sea horses and boat races . . . swinging boats, shooting galleries and Aunt Sallies".[21] On hot summer evenings, literally tens of thousands of people paraded along the Esplanade and the jetty at Glenelg. Bands gave concerts from the jetty and in the gardens surrounding the Town Hall. Hucksters shouted each other down on the broad beach, and the steam whirlygigs and sideshows tussled for the attention of the crowds.

Glenelg had established its reputation on the simplest entertainments, yet the simplest of them all, swimming, was hedged in by moral outrage or caged in with bars. Glenelg had forbidden all swimming by 1858, because "public decency is outraged by men bathing within the limits of the Town of Glenelg".[22] Five years later the By-laws were relaxed to allow bathing so long as it was before eight in the morning or after 12 midnight. If bathers outraged public decency by the light of day, then apparently "Bathing Vans" did not. These were allowed on the beach in the daytime by 1870, but it is not clear whether or not bathers were allowed to leave the vans and thus offend decency. In the nineties it was legal to bathe during the day, but only within certain reserved areas, separate for males and females. To approach any member of the opposite sex wearing a bathing costume, to within 12 yards, was to incur a serious fine.

"The most extensive Natatorium in the world"[23] was built in 1875, and the problems of outraged decency came to an end. The "Natatorium" consisted of bars driven into the sea bottom at frequent intervals so as to enclose the swimmers in a large cage. The whole area was discretely boarded up, and the sexes were separated to either side of the jetty. There were dressing cubicles, but showers were an extra expense. In the men's baths, 110 dressing rooms covered an area 180 feet by 500 feet. It was recommended that hot salt water showers, at 1/6 each, should not be followed by fresh water showers, though these too were available. It was thought that the salt should remain on the body, and one should dress over it, to obtain the maximum health benefit.[24] The cost of using this "Natatorium" was £3 a year, or 6d a bath. The 7.00 a.m. "Bathers' Train" from Adelaide offered a combined train and bath ticket for 1/-. Despite the success of the "Natatorium", many people were a little unsure of a past-time which had been so recently considered immoral. The following rules, from a tourist pamphlet on Glenelg, clearly demonstrate this.[25]

1. **Don't go in the water too often.**
2. **Don't stay in the water too long. (Fifteen minutes is quite long enough).**
3. **Don't go out too far from the shore.**
4. **Don't go in the water when the waves are breaking roughly.**
5. **Don't make yourself tired by trying to swim too much.**
6. **Don't allow children's heads to be uncovered when the sun is strong.**

These rules, combined with By-law 40 which demanded covering so as to "prevent exposure of the person", left little space for the average citizen to enjoy a simple swim in the sea.

THE 1890s

During the late 1880s, drought and mismanagement had caused a collapse in the financial boom, and Adelaide was beginning to feel the effects. The great depression that followed brought a dramatic fall in the growth of the city. By 1896 Adelaide had suffered an entire decade of stagnation in building, for practically no new areas had been added to the area of urban Adelaide. (See Adelaide Urban Area Map 1903, page 44). In 1891, the city of Adelaide's population had fallen by 1.7% on the figure of 10 years earlier. The depression did not completely kill Glenelg's boom but there was no expansion in area under subdivision during the 1890s (see Map D, Glenelg Subdivision 1915, page 48), but by the turn of the century a large business and residential area near the centre of the old town had developed. The 1900s found Glenelg an established and highly popular seaside resort.[26]

The photograph (D1) shows Glenelg's main street lined with large elegant hotels, shops and business houses. Crowds had continued to come during the hot summers of the depression and the recovery of the following years. On one Saturday in 1896, 17,000 people visited Glenelg by train, and many stayed until quite late in the evening. Even on an ordinary week-day evening Glenelg attracted thousands of visitors. Thursday, February 13, 1896, drew a record crowd to Glenelg, where among the usual entertainments of shooting galleries, merry-go-rounds and steamer trips, Blondin, the great acrobat, performed balancing tricks.[27] Steamer trips to Port Adelaide and Kangaroo Island left the Glenelg jetty regularly.

An evening's entertainment early in 1893 typifies the sort of attraction which gave Glenelg its fame. This particular evening, in January 1893, was

Photograph D1, looking down Jetty Road, the business and commercial centre, from outside the Pier Hotel. Taken about 1900. *(See Map D, p. 48)*
(Burgess Cyclopedia of S.A.)

reported in full detail by the newspapers. It was a "Continental Evening", in which a concert was given by three bands. As a variation on the normal theme of concerts, the Adelaide Glee Club performed part songs and glees from the deck of a steamer as it floated near the jetty. The idea was that "the chorus across the water makes beautiful effects",[28] for the spectators who lined the jetty and shore. During the intervals between songs, Mr. Sctaro's string band played numbers from the seaward end of the jetty, and the Holdfast Model Band played from the illuminated balcony of the Town Hall. Throughout the concert, steam launches plied about the jetty taking passengers, and a steamer demonstrated a "flash light" by illuminating the coast some five miles away. Special late trains took the last of the visitors away at 11 o'clock at night.

Thus by the turn of the century, Glenelg was a major suburban town of Adelaide and a very popular seaside resort. The local residents were still very proud of their mansions. Tourist publications of the 1890s had as many pictures of "local mansions and villas" as they had pages of writing on all other subjects.[29] However, the days when Glenelg could be called a marine retreat had gone with the arrival of the railways and the great rise in popularity in the 1870s. Glenelg was still a distinct and separate community in relation to Adelaide, with a character and fame of its own, but the turn of the century saw the peak of Glenelg's fame and the beginning of its slow absorption into the homogeneity of suburban Adelaide and obscurity.

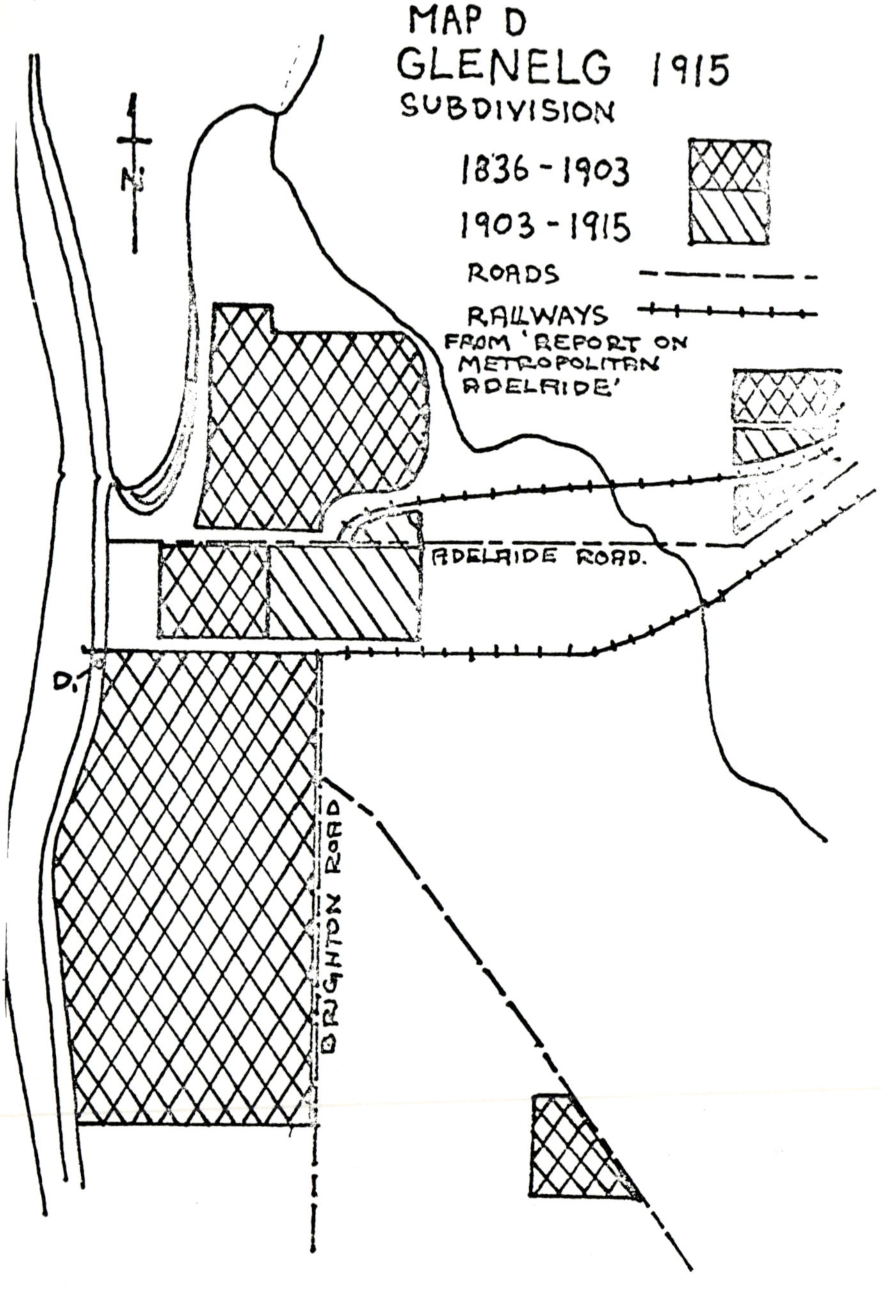
MAP D
GLENELG 1915
SUBDIVISION
1836 - 1903
1903 - 1915
ROADS
RAILWAYS
FROM 'REPORT ON METROPOLITAN ADELAIDE'
N
ADELAIDE ROAD.
BRIGHTON ROAD
D.

CHAPTER FOUR

COMMUNITY LIFE IN VICTORIAN GLENELG

VICTORIAN Glenelg was a unique self-contained community of people, as well as the major holiday centre of Adelaide. The vast annual migration of holiday makers had an enormous effect on the small town, but it was ultimately to its three thousand residents that Glenelg looked for its permanent character. This community grew rapidly and changed during the Victorian era, but still many of its characteristic features remained the same throughout, and they can be seen in all aspects of Glenelg's society.

HIGH SOCIETY

Glenelg was founded by high society. The wealthy businessmen and Parliamentarians who had built their mansions at Glenelg in the 1840s and 1850s had literally created the town by providing the only employment in the area that could justify such a concentration of population. The mansions dominated every perspective of Glenelg in the middle of the nineteenth century, and the social and economic orders they created were to underlie the development of Glenelg until the turn of the century. The census of 1861[1] clearly reveals the pattern of this mansion society. The proportion of men occupied in traditionally middle and upper class professions at Glenelg exceeded that of Adelaide by nearly 40%[2]. Those who derived their income from "independent means" constituted 1.8% at Glenelg, but only .5% at Adelaide city. Thus Glenelg had a disproportionately large upper class of men in comparison to Adelaide city, the business and commercial centre of the colony. The proportion of women who worked as teachers at Glenelg also indicates that a larger proportion of upper class women lived there than in Adelaide.[3] The working classes at Glenelg depended heavily on the mansions, for one-fifth of all male residents were employed directly or indirectly in maintaining, staffing and supplying them[4]. The biggest single area for the employment of women was as domestic staff or tutors, and these accounted for one quarter of the entire population of women and girls in Glenelg. Only 14% of Adelaide's women by comparison were employed as domestics or teachers. Not only was there a very high proportion of domestic servants at Glenelg, they were also servants typical of the upper class rather than the normal middle class household servants. This is indicated by the fact that there were more than three times the number of male servants at Glenelg than there were at Adelaide.[5] Men had to be paid higher wages and were considered the servants of a richer class. Thus Glenelg's economic community was dominated by the mansions in 1861, and although this dominance decreased with the years, it remained a fundamental fact of the community life.

The trains and increased popularity of the 1870s brought many changes to Glenelg. However, the 1881 census revealed that in 20 years the changes had not proved to be fundamental. Glenelg's upper class professions[6] still accounted for more of the population than they did in Adelaide. The economy still relied heavily on employment in the mansions, with 16.5% of women as domestic servants, compared to 10% in Adelaide, but this was a big decrease from the 21.1% thus employed at Glenelg in 1861. The proportion of men employed as servants dropped below that of Adelaide. The real changes had come in the widening of employment opportunities for the working class rather than in decreasing the importance of the upper class minority. In fact, almost the reverse occurred; as Glenelg expanded and filled out as a complete community, its pride in the famous and dignified owners of the mansions and patrons of society, if anything grew.

Moseley Square and Jetty Road in the 1870s — Railways and popularity

(Burgess Cyclopedia of S.A.)

Mr. Rugless, a porter on the Glenelg trains for 47 years, and thus definitely a member of the working class, remembers those aristocrats of Glenelg:

> In those days it was a common sight to see men in their top hats and flowing coats ride their horses along the old Diagonal Road . . . Men like Sir John (Morphett), and the Bickfords, William Pile, Sir Thomas Elder, Sir Herbert Phillips, the Duffields, and the Jessups all went about with a casual air of superiority, but they never-the-less were good men sent along by providence to steer South Australia along the road to progress.[7]

Above and below: Glenelg mansions dominated the society as much as they did the skyline in the Victorian era. These are two that survive today
(Author's photograph)

It was an aristocracy which could claim some of the most dignified men in the whole colony, who were remembered fondly by the citizens of Glenelg for their eccentricities. Sir H. E. F. Young, the Governor, often stayed at the Governor's Residence during the summer, and

> could be seen any morning in the season emerging thence with a bath towel over his shoulders bound for a matutional dip at the mouth of the Patawalonga Creek.[8]

These men exercised an abnormally large economic power in the community, and this, in some ways, increased the social gap between the classes. Coachmen would ride their "shining black broughams and carriages . . . sitting up rigidly at attention as if afraid they would fall off their safe perches."[9] The Smiths, Sowards, Hills, Hopes and Beyers built villas at Glenelg, which Ziegler still boasted proudly of in the late 1920s.

Society was comfortably ordered, and it was always better if this order was acknowledged and respected. Order even extended to favourite seats on the train: (they) "showed their resentment in no uncertain manner if anyone chanced to occupy these special places."[10]

Although mansion society continued to dominate the economic and social community at Glenelg, deeper changes, to become apparent later, were undermining the whole situation. By 1881 these features were showing marked changes. A distinct increase in the number of young men at Glenelg was evident, over and above the increase in the same age group for Adelaide (15 to 30 year olds). The predominance of young single women at Glenelg was then parallelled by Adelaide instead of contrasted to it as in previous decades. Middle aged married men also had lost their predominance in the population structure. All of these trends are further confirmed by the 1891 census, which gives Adelaide and Glenelg rather similar population structures. These changes in the population can all be explained by the gradual growth of Glenelg's economy and the change away from a mansion-dominated society.

The railways and popularity not only brought fame to Glenelg, but, more importantly, brought many more employment opportunities.

Glenelg, in 1881, no longer relied heavily on the mansions for employment. The new population structure reflected the changes in a greater proportion of young working men. As Glenelg's economic and social community became more diversified, the old social structures were undermined, and the role played by high society became less important.

Glenelg was also beginning to play a new role which was to prove to be the most lasting of all the changes. Commuter traffic between the city's business, commercial and industrial centres and Glenelg had been made possible for the first time by the trains. During the 1880s, this traffic was important enough to require two trains each day being set aside for commuter traffic alone. A workman's ticket was issued for these trains only, and it cut the normal cost in half.[12] Although Glenelg was certainly not a dormitory suburb for the city of Adelaide during the Victorian era, the trend which was to result in this fate some 40 years later, had already begun.

A LOCUS OF COMMUNITY LIFE

Four points of interest may be taken to deliniate a locus of the community life in Victorian Glenelg. The place of religion in most communities of the era was an important indication of the social and economic stratas. As Glenelg was in the majority an upper class community, religious practice was particularly important in community life. Education was also particularly valued in an upper

The Roman Catholic Church was built in 1926, costing £30,000 and seating 700. It illustrates the late but vigorous growth of this religion at Glenelg

(Author's photograph)

class society, and therefore was an important feature of Victorian Glenelg. An analysis of the offences committed at Glenelg over an 18 month period in the 1880s helps to balance the picture of Glenelg with a view of its less socially accepted facets. However, perhaps the most revealing point of interest is found in the types of entertainment sought by the permanent residents at Glenelg.

(1) Religion

For over a half a century the mansion society of Glenelg made the little town the stronghold of the establishment and also the stronghold of religious

St. Peter's Anglican Church was built in 1881, in the reserve set aside for it in Light's plan

(Author's photograph)

The Congregational Church on Jetty Road. The last of three on the site, it was built in 1880 (Author's photograph)

orthodoxy. In South Australia the orthodox religions were the Church of England, Methodists and Congregationalists. The 1871 census shows that these religions of the establishment accounted for a far higher proportion of the religious community at Glenelg than at Adelaide. The biggest difference between the two towns is apparent in the very large proportion of Congregationalists at Glenelg (18.4%

compared with 6.2% for Adelaide city), and in the unusually small proportion of Roman Catholics. The Congregationalists may be explained by the many business and professional men living at Glenelg, and working in Adelaide. Most of Glenelg's Roman Catholics were women. This may be accounted for by the high proportion of Irish women, most of whom must have emigrated from Ireland under the massive government assistance plans of the 1850s to become domestic servants in South Australia. Therefore the small proportion of Catholics in Glenelg were probably of the working class, although a certain number of them consisted of the business men and upper classes as they did in all Victorian communities. The higher proportion of Catholics in Adelaide was probably due to the higher proportion of working men. The Primitive Church and the Baptists were also relatively unimportant at Glenelg, again because of the smaller working class.

Glenelg's first church was built in the same year that saw the opening of its second hotel. The Congregational Church was opened in 1848, and by the 1880s the church had been rebuilt twice, each time more gloriously. The Church which remains today in Jetty Road (see photograph p. 55) eventually cost £14,000, which was equal to half the cost of the entire jetty and its port facilities. Its opulent design still dominates the main street of Glenelg, a testimony both to Glenelg's wealth and religious devotion. In 1852, St. Peter's, Church of England, was opened, on the site in the square provided for that specific church in Light's original plan of Glenelg (see Map C, p. 21). In 1881, when Glenelg was reaching the peak of its prosperity, this church was rebuilt into the edifice which survives today. Therefore, even before the town was proclaimed a municipality in 1855, two churches of the establishment had built their solid foundations in Glenelg's soil. A Methodist Chapel was built within a year of that date.

The census figures for 1891 begin to show changes in the religious composition of the community. The proportion of Roman Catholics had risen since 1871, as had the proportion of the Primitive Church and Baptists. These were the sects associated with the working class, which, as has been shown previously, was also increasing. The proportion of Congregationalists showed a marked fall. However, despite these changes towards more working class religious sects, Glenelg was still dominated by the beliefs of the establishment when compared with Adelaide. A Birthplace analysis for 1881 and 1891 showed that although both Adelaide and Glenelg had increasingly homogeneous populations, the Australian and British born population at Glenelg always accounted for a larger proportion than at Adelaide. These national groups contained most of the people considered to be upper class. Perhaps the most significant change caused by the growth of the non-establishment religious groups in the latter part of the century was that the fourth new church to be built in Glenelg was Roman Catholic (see photograph p. 53).

(2) The Schools

Victorian schooling was largely a private affair. Until the Education Act of 1875 when a State school was established, schools at Glenelg existed wherever a schoolmaster or mistress hung his or her hat. A unique feature of Glenelg complicated this situation. The 1861 census showed that 101 students lived at Glenelg, as did 10 teachers. Yet in 1861, there was only one licenced school at Glenelg, with 36 boys and 18 girls being taught by one teacher. Thus, nearly half of the students at Glenelg either learned at home with governesses or boarded in the large private schools of the city. Education had always been the prerogative of the well-to-do, and such a large number of private scholars indicated the extent of Glenelg's rich homes. The aim of education, even in Mr. Caterer's licenced school, was to produce "finished" ladies and gentlemen. In Tremere, Mr. Caterer taught 88 children in 1858[13] the fundamentals of reading, writing, arithmetic and grammar. Of the students, 64 studied geography, 22 history, 28 a foreign language, and only eight mathematics. All the students had to learn singing, and half of them studied "Natural Philosophy". The Inspector commented that Mr. Caterer was "amongst the foremost teachers of the colony", but he was only "partially successful at Glenelg"[14] and in 1860 was forced to leave because of the lack of patronage.

"Tremere", on Anzac Highway. This mansion served, amongst other things, as Glenelg's Town Hall and Mr. Caterer's School

(Author's photograph)

Glenelg was given its first school house in 1870, when the Council established and subsidised a new school. One hundred and ten pupils were registered, but the average daily attendance was only 46. The children attended that school for an average of 96 of the 229 schooldays in a year. The Government took over the school in 1876, but the annual attendance was still lower than it had been at Mr. Caterer's school 20 years before. Mr. Caterer was back in Glenelg by 1890 and established a school in the old Government cottage.

A typical programme of the school prize-giving evening at this time gives a fascinating insight into the type of subjects taught at these schools. The programme [15] included:

1. *Chairman's Address.*
2. *Overture.*
3. *Chorus: "Hail Smiling Morn".*
4. *Recitation: "Scene from the tragedy of Cato".*
5. *Descriptive Fantasia: "When Johnny Comes Marching Home".*
6. *Recitations.*
7. *Chorus: "Wet sheet and a flowing sea".*
8. *Recitation: "The Charge of the Light Brigade".*
9. *Recitation: "The Bashful Bachelor".*
10. *Chorus of Old Lang Syne.*

GOD SAVE THE QUEEN.

(3) Crime

Constable C. P. Badman was appointed to Glenelg in 1865 as the town's first policeman. He was withdrawn three years later and replaced by a constable with a more fortunate name, Allchurch. Glenelg had waited a quarter of a century for Badman, and even then the Councillors complained that he was not sufficient for a town of such a size. An analysis of offences committed at Glenelg between the middle of 1881 and the end of 1882[16] gives a revealing picture. Although the greatest number of convictions was for drunkenness (40 convictions of the 157 total), only one person was convicted as an inebriate, so the drunkenness may be attributed to the fact that the town was a resort. The next biggest class of convictions (21) was breaking Corporation By-laws, though it is not clear what By-laws were broken. "Breach of Education" comes a close third (with 18 offenders) and almost as many (16) were convicted of disorderly conduct. These too might be attributed to the holiday atmosphere of Glenelg. With all the drunkenness and disorderly conduct, it is surprising that in 18 months only five people were convicted of assault, four of indecency, and five for larceny. Although 186 dogs were registered, only four people were tried under the "Dog Act" and three people for cruelty to animals. The distinction between larceny and unlawful possession is not made clear, but three people were convicted for the latter. High spirits also seemed to be the cause of many of the small scale offences recorded. Three people were convicted for "furious riding", two for obstruction of the police, three for wilful damage, two for lunacy, one for attempting to start a bushfire, and one person was convicted for "personating the police." None of these offences were particularly reprehensible or indicative of an unhealthy community. Those which were, occurred only infrequently. Two people were convicted for neglect of children, one was tried under the Health Act, and three were arrested as "Rogues and Vagabonds". Only one person was tried under the Masters and Servants Act, and one was convicted of forgery.

(4) Entertainment

The entertainment sought by the Glenelg residents shows a hidden streak of morbid sentimentality and racist bigotry which is not apparent in other facets of life in Glenelg. These features, however, were probably typical of Victorian Adelaide as well.

The holidaying crowds who invaded Glenelg during the summer months brought with them the peculiar sorts of entertainment described in the previous chapter. These entertainments were typical of any seaside resort in the world and were concentrated along the beach, on the jetty, and in the baths (see photograph, p. 60). These entertainments were under tents during the summer season and tended to disappear with the crowds in the winter.

The thousands of people who lived permanently in Glenelg sought a very different type of entertainment as well as those of the resort. Recitals, lectures, balls and concerts were held throughout the year in the Institute Building, which later became a part of the Town Hall (see photograph p. 59). These were the only sorts of public entertainment available at Glenelg and were usually presented by an "Amateur Society" in order to raise funds for some building project. Often a bazaar would be held during the day and be followed at night by a concert. These "Promenade Concerts" present a curiously mixed picture of the Victorian mentality. Amongst songs that displayed gross sentimentality, such as "Kiss Me Mother Kiss Your Darling", "Keep One Little Kiss For Me", and "Little Sister's Gone To Sleep", were mixed racist songs called "Nigger Farces".[17]

The Glenelg Town Hall. Originally built as the Glenelg Institute, it has been the centre of Glenelg's entertainment for over a century. Its hall housed many of the lectures and entertainments discussed in this chapter, and its great balcony was the scene of the open air concerts described in Chapter 3

The Beach — a scene typical of Victorian Glenelg. The Town Hall and the Pier Hotel dominate the background. Note that few people are actually swimming
(Burgess Cyclopedia of S.A.)

In 1929, Glenelg held a carnival that was typical of the 1920s form of entertainment. An advertisement described the attractions as:

> exquisite dancing girls, magnificent nobles and Hareem slaves and over all the subtle breath of an exotic perfume-laden breeze. This is Persia, and this will be Glenelg during the Great Carnival.[1]

Photograph E1, looking from Moseley Square to the Patawalonga, 1928
(S.A. Archives)

When, in 1930, an enormous complex of round-abouts, side-shows and, over all, an enormous big dipper were erected at Glenelg, the crowds that came could have challenged the Victorian era's records. (See photograph p. 65.) This was called Luna Park, and five years after its opening it was dismantled and taken to Melbourne, where it remains today as one of that much larger city's major tourist attractions. Glenelg was still very much the centre of all Adelaide's holiday activities in the 1920s, and although the town was growing rapidly and the days of a mansion society were long past, it remained a unique, self-contained and proud community. Cinderella did not leave the Ball, the Ball left Cinderella.

ADELAIDE'S URBAN REVOLUTION

While Glenelg was enjoying its Indian summer, the greater city of Adelaide was undergoing major changes. The foundation of the city had been laid with a central nucleus for business, commerce and administration, and with a number of small scattered settlements along major roads, at the port and near rivers. Since then the city had grown radially. Settlements had grown outwards from the original scattered townships, following the roads to the city and the water courses. Travel was lengthy and difficult in the days of horse cabs, horse buses and poor dirt roads. Therefore, employment opportunities and town services were necessarily concentrated in this radial pattern. Even in 1915, and as late as the 1930s this radial pattern is evident in the urban growth of Adelaide. (See Urban Area Maps

1915 and 1937). The conditions which promoted this century-long pattern of development were crucial to Glenelg's function as a seaside resort.

Glenelg was on the terminus of one of the city's biggest arterial roads and one of its first railways. The great urban growth that Adelaide experienced in the 1880s and later had put an enormous pressure on local food supplies,

Glenelg's Luna Park in 1930

(S.A. Archives)

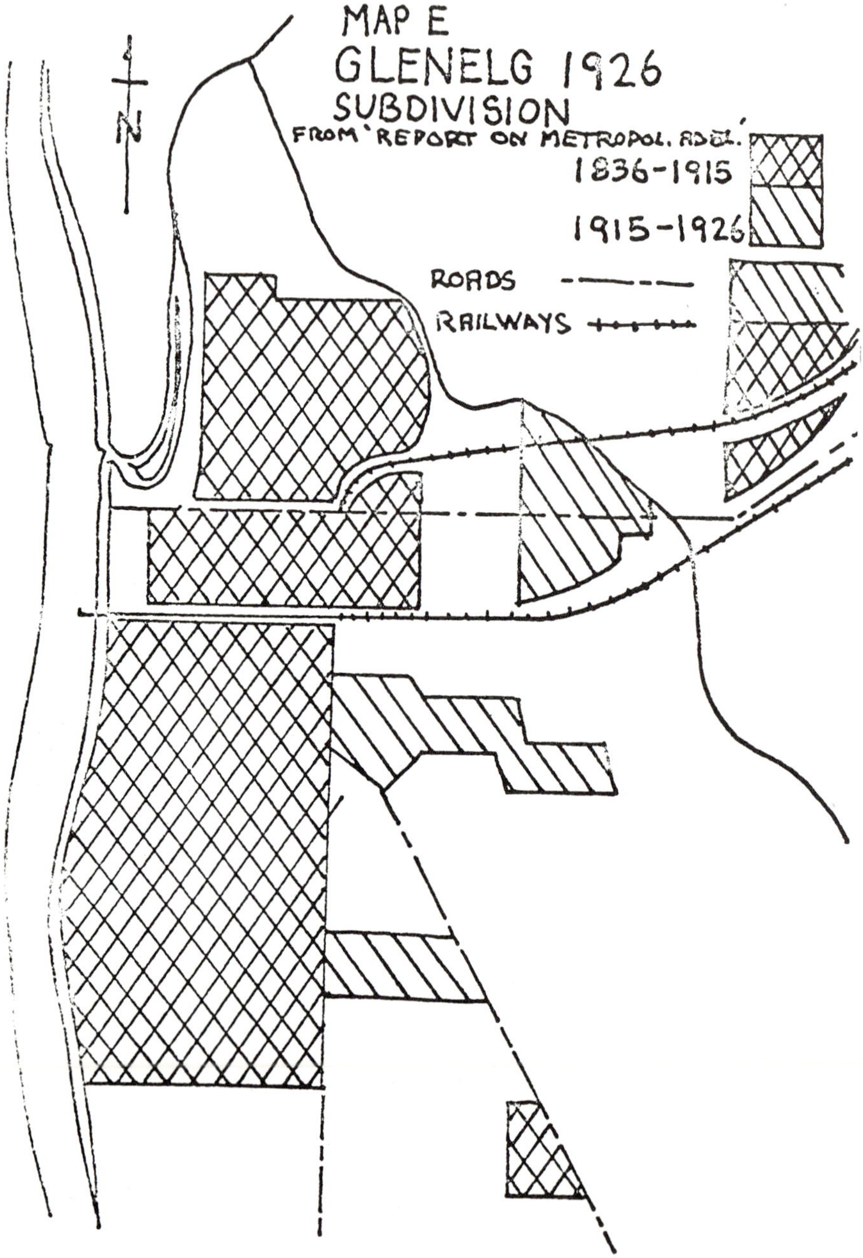
MAP E
GLENELG 1926
SUBDIVISION
FROM 'REPORT ON METROPOL. ADEL.'
N
1836-1915
1915-1926
ROADS
RAILWAYS

which came largely from the dairy farms, orchards and market gardens of the Adelaide plains to the south. The Glenelg Road was a major artery in the growing body of Adelaide and constituted one of the main arms of its radial development. It was far easier to travel to Glenelg than to any other part of the coast during the nineteenth century, yet Glenelg remained buffered from the main areas of

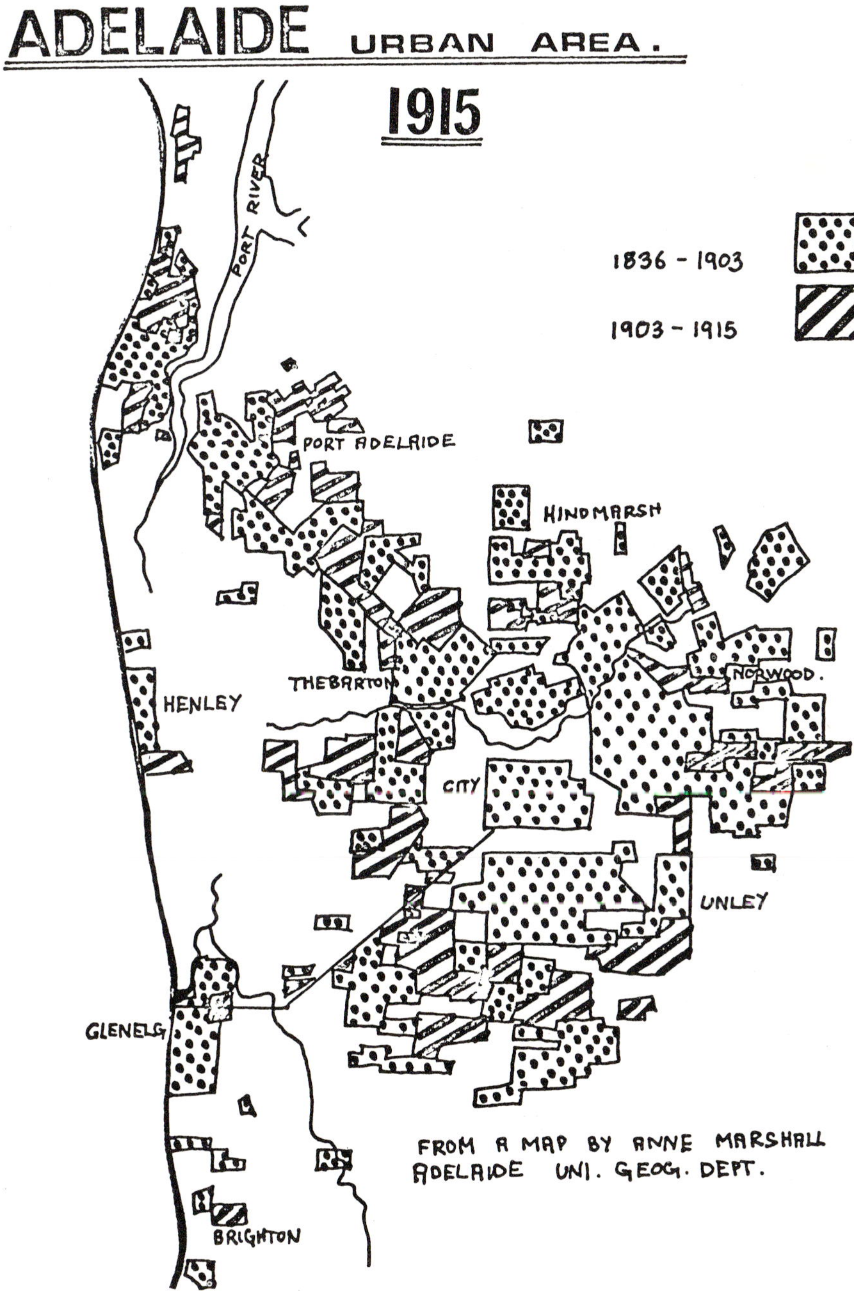

This old mansi

separateness was
had already begu
Car own
century, but in
90,000 cars regis
advanced admini
In 1923 bitumino

Photograph F1
sprawl of the
a peculiar mi

urban growth b
most accessible a
the entire 20 mil
forced nearly ev
on short holiday
of its attraction,
keep Adelaide's

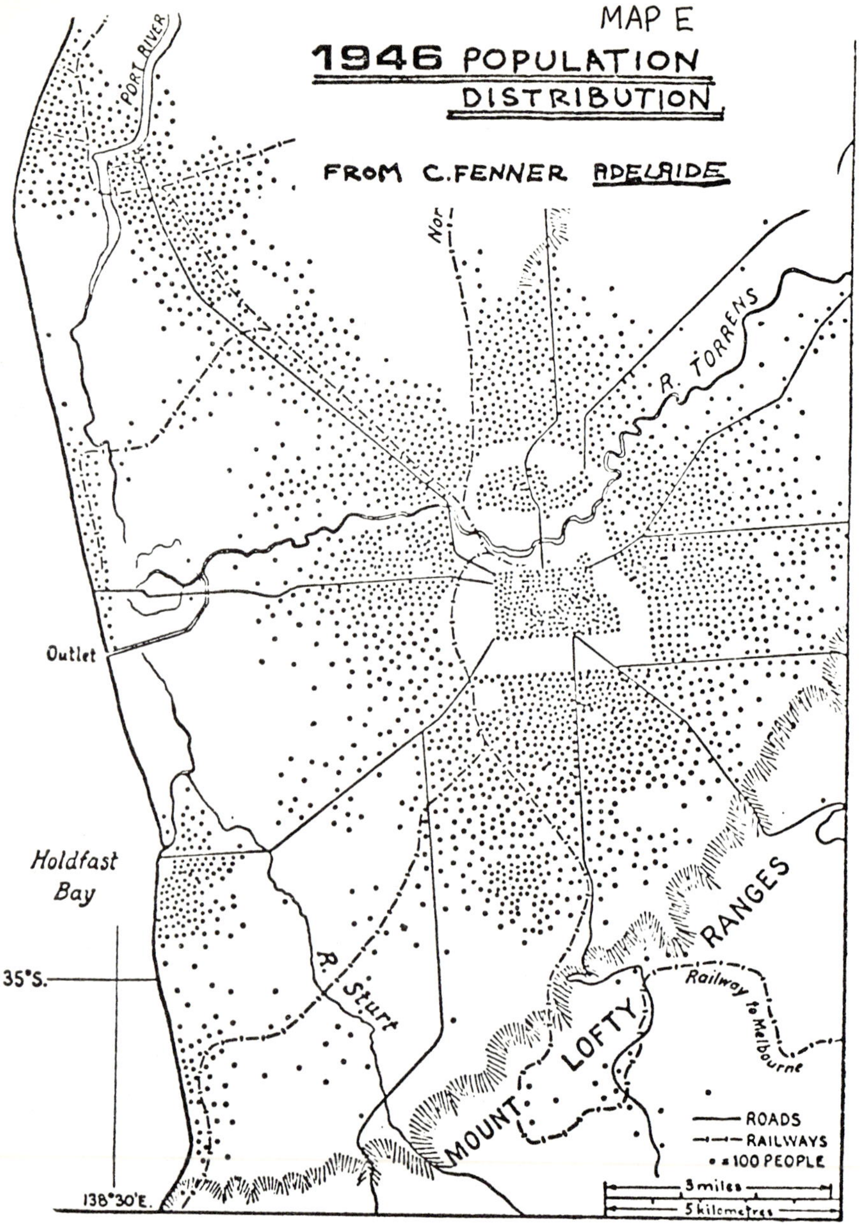

unemployed. All excess spending had to be drastically cut. When Adelaide pulled its purse strings, Glenelg was strangled.

When the suburban sprawl reached Glenelg in the 1940s, it brought with it the final indignity. The houses which filled vast new areas in neat and compact

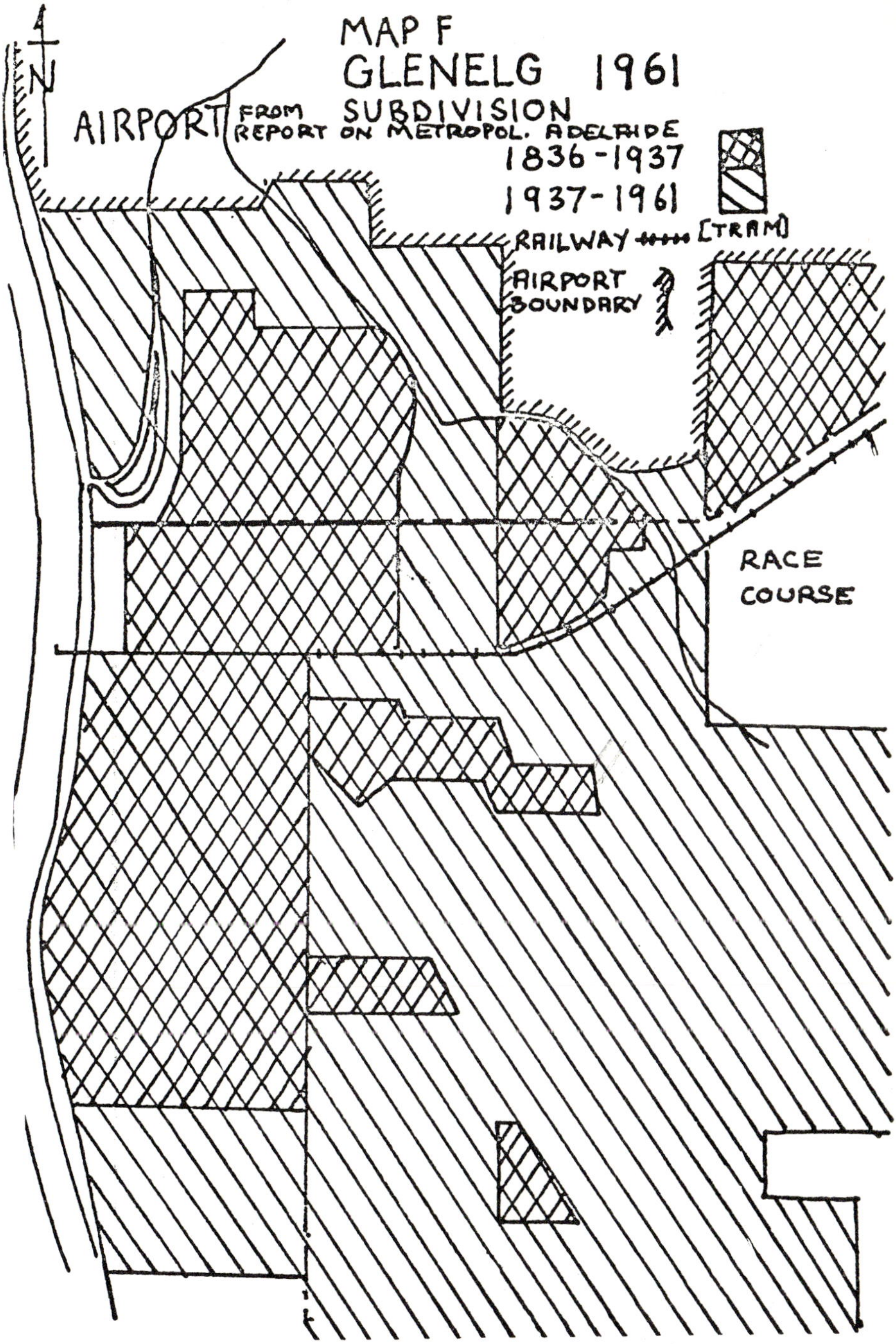
MAP F
GLENELG 1961
SUBDIVISION
FROM
REPORT ON METROPOL. ADELAIDE
1836-1937
1937-1961
RAILWAY
[TRAM]
AIRPORT BOUNDARY
AIRPORT
N
RACE COURSE

rows were identical with those built anywhere else in Adelaide at that time. (See photographs p. 68). The suburban sprawl allowed an amazingly low density of people to cover an amazingly large area with houses, concrete, and bitumen. (See Map E). Thus Glenelg suffered the humiliation of being like any other part of the whole city of Adelaide. The "collective attempt at private living"[3] produced the conformity to a romantic stereotype and buried the old town and character of Glenelg forever.

MAP(S) F

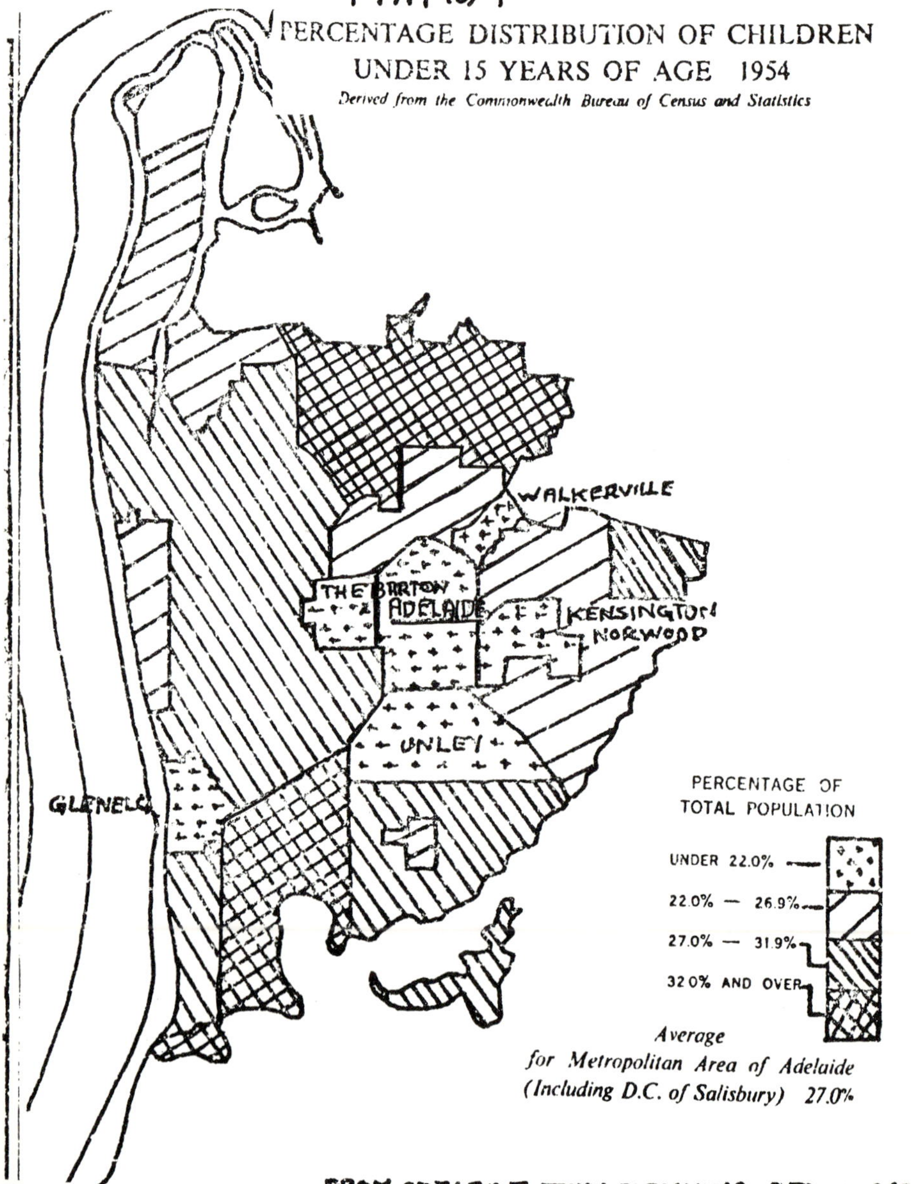

FROM ADELAIDE TOWN PLANNING REPORT 1962

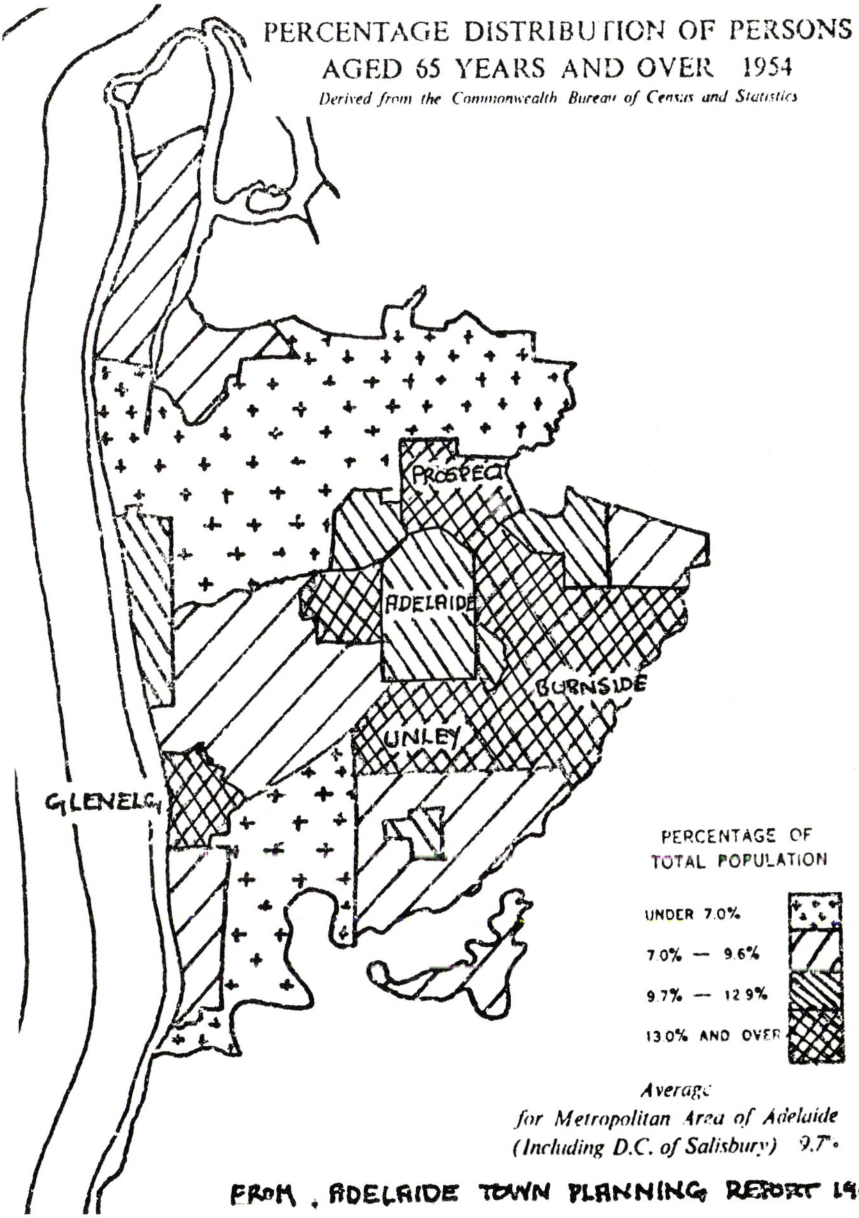

FROM . ADELAIDE TOWN PLANNING REPORT 1962

MAP G

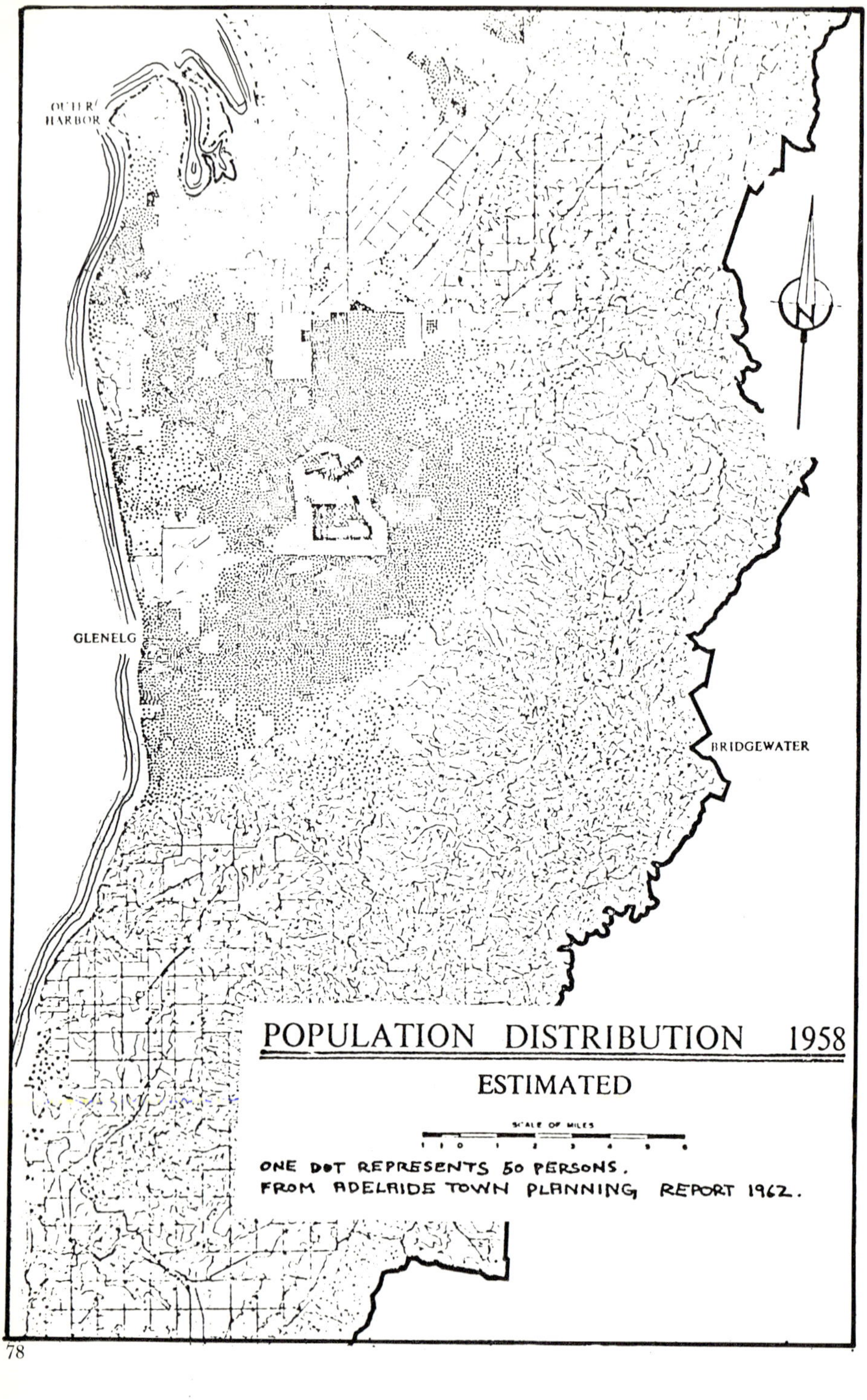
OUTER HARBOR
GLENELG
BRIDGEWATER
N
POPULATION DISTRIBUTION 1958
ESTIMATED
SCALE OF MILES
ONE DOT REPRESENTS 50 PERSONS.
FROM ADELAIDE TOWN PLANNING REPORT 1962.

THE LITTLE OLD SUBURB

By the mid 1950s, Adelaide's urban sprawl had nearly covered the entire Adelaide plains, and Glenelg had been completely engulfed in suburbia. The building boom of the late 1940s had pushed the suburbs up to the foothills in the east and south and to the beach in the west. (See Map G). Glenelg was no longer a town but a mere suburb in the city of Adelaide. In 1948 a freak storm destroyed its jetty and thus removed one of its last claims to a unique position amongst the many seaside suburbs of Adelaide.

Glenelg was regarded as one of Adelaide's quaint little old suburbs during the 1950s and 1960s. However, it had gained a new uniqueness in losing the old one in the urban revolution. Glenelg became an island of old houses and mansions in a sea of small stereotyped urban houses. This, and the fact that the Anzac Highway allowed very fast commuting to the city centre, began to give Glenelg a new role in the new and much larger urban community. Adelaide had used up nearly all its available flat land for building on, yet its population continued to grow. Glenelg's old houses and convenient situation were well suited to conversion into flats. Flats had been built as early as 1878 in Glenelg, but it was not until the 1930s and 1940s that many new ones were built along the sea-front and most of the old mansions were converted into flats by partitioning and by adding lean-to's. (See photographs, ps. 69, 72, 73). Young couples could live in these flats and drive to work every day on the Anzac Highway. However, the majority of tenants were old couples who wanted to live near the beach for health reasons or who needed cheap accommodation.

Glenelg in the Victorian era had been a very young community with a far larger percentage of children than the city of Adelaide. This is typical of a newly established and vigorously growing community. However, as the new suburbs of the twentieth century grew, Glenelg's population became dominated by its old people, as did many of the other old suburbs. (See Map F). In large cities like Adelaide it is usual for the inner city areas to die as the youth of the city moves to the newer suburbs. Glenelg was relatively unique in sharing the fate of the inner city. Young couples could not build their homes where land was already developed, so Glenelg was left to the flat tenants and to the aged. Large old buildings were easily converted into private hospitals which could take advantage of the sea air and the quick communications with Adelaide. Glenelg became, in more ways than one, Adelaide's oldest suburb. (See Map M, p. 83.) Note that all the hospitals at Glenelg are relatively small and privately owned).

As an old suburb, Glenelg did have certain advantages over the new suburbs that surrounded it. Its business and commercial centre was far more highly developed than any of the newer centres such as Marion and Brighton. Its Jetty Road was one of the four largest shopping centres in the whole metropolitan area. (See Map L, p. 83.) These shops provided specialist services such as tailoring, department stores and the type of small businesses that only thrive amongst specialist shops. It was the closest centre to the southern suburbs around Marion where the greatest urban and market expansion had occurred. It served an area that was restricted to residential buildings (see Map J), and which provided one of the biggest buying markets in Adelaide. Until a large shopping complex was built at Marion to tap this rapidly expanding market, it had looked to Glenelg as well as to Adelaide for its business and shopping needs.

With business success, Glenelg became a valuable business investment. By 1960, Jetty Road was worth from £24,000 to £100,000 per acre, and this unimproved land value was exceeded only by the centre of the city. (See Map H). Large areas

Glenelg, home for the old and the sick. Above, old citizens rest in the shade of the Town Hall verandah. Below is one of the many private hospitals

(Author's photographs)

of the foreshore were considered fashionable to live in, and they were classed by the 1961 Town Planning Committee report as a "good class area". (See Map I). Their unimproved land value of from £12,000 to £24,000 per acre indicated that the foreshore was highly developed. The continuous row of holiday flats, subdivided mansions, rest homes and private hospitals that lined the foreshore in 1970 bears witness to the degree of development. Although Glenelg could never regain its fame and character as a seaside resort, it did achieve a new burst of popularity as a pleasant residential suburb in the late 1950s and the early 1960s. In 1959, the traffic carried by Anzac Highway, the old Glenelg Road, indicated the growing importance of Glenelg as a residential suburb. However, the suburbs to its south were growing at a much faster rate than Glenelg could maintain. Glenelg was limited to a very small area (1200 acres), and the Development Plan of the Town Planning Committee estimated that its population would decrease during the period 1961 to 1971.

MAP H.

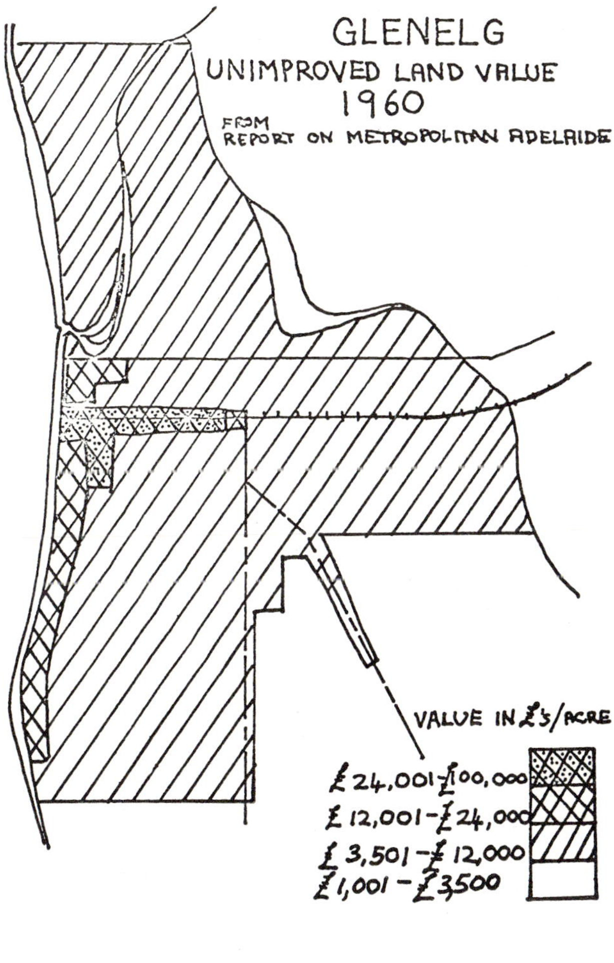

MAP I.

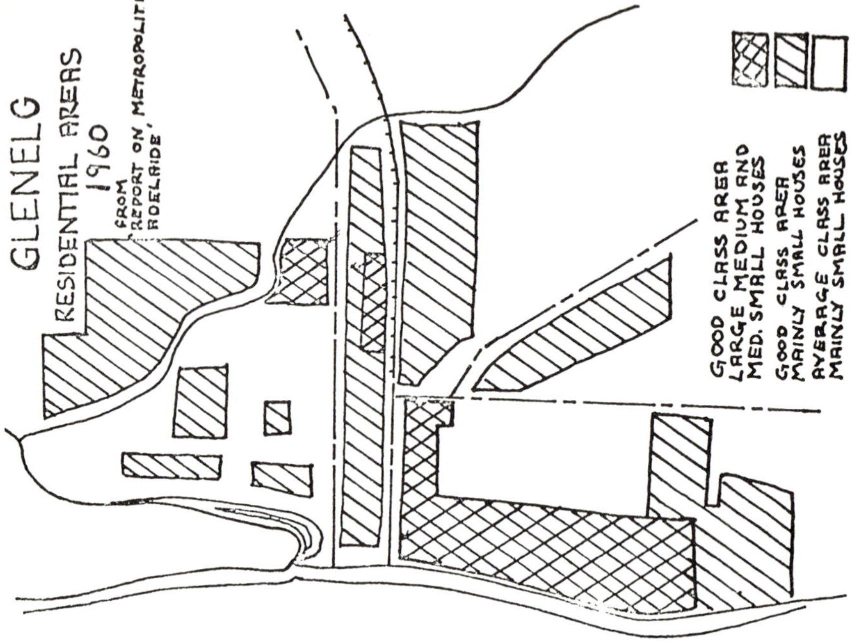
GLENELG
RESIDENTIAL AREAS
1960
FROM REPORT ON METROPOLITAN ADELAIDE'
GOOD CLASS AREA LARGE MEDIUM AND MED. SMALL HOUSES
GOOD CLASS AREA MAINLY SMALL HOUSES
AVERAGE CLASS AREA MAINLY SMALL HOUSES

MAP J.

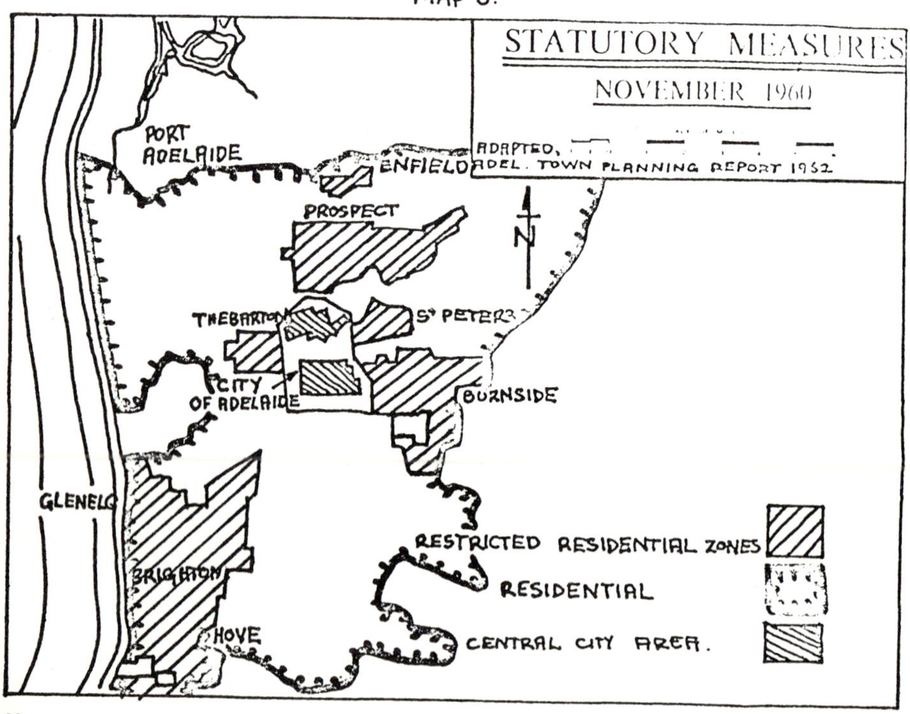
STATUTORY MEASURES
NOVEMBER 1960
ADAPTED, ADEL. TOWN PLANNING REPORT 1952
PORT ADELAIDE
ENFIELD
PROSPECT
N
THEBARTON
St PETERS
CITY OF ADELAIDE
BURNSIDE
GLENELG
BRIGHTON
HOVE
RESTRICTED RESIDENTIAL ZONES
RESIDENTIAL
CENTRAL CITY AREA.

MAPS L. + M.

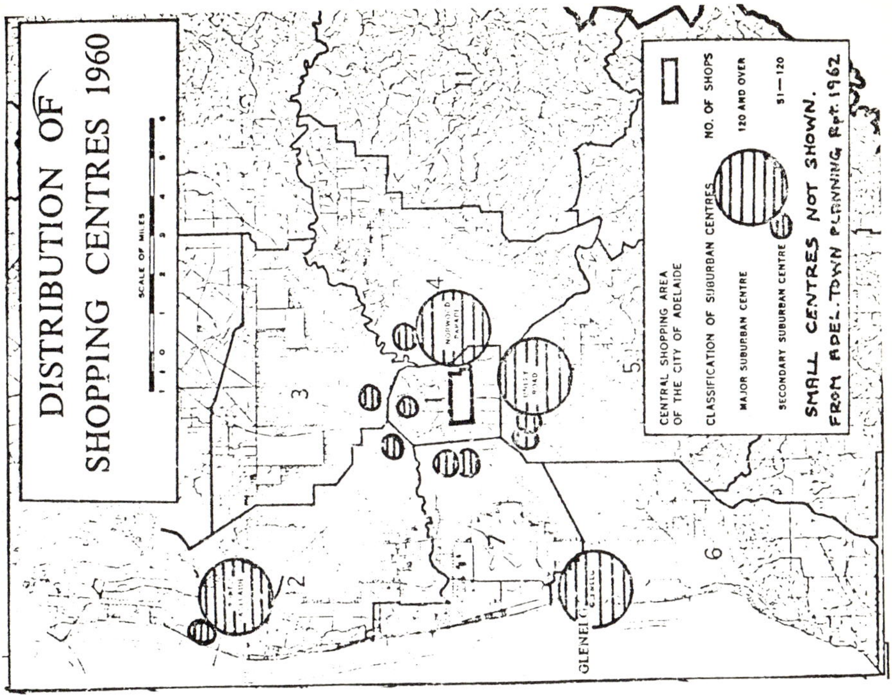
DISTRIBUTION OF
SHOPPING CENTRES 1960
SCALE OF MILES
CENTRAL SHOPPING AREA
OF THE CITY OF ADELAIDE
CLASSIFICATION OF SUBURBAN CENTRES
NO. OF SHOPS
MAJOR SUBURBAN CENTRE
120 AND OVER
SECONDARY SUBURBAN CENTRE
51—120
SMALL CENTRES NOT SHOWN.
FROM ADEL. TOWN PLANNING Rpt. 1962
GLENELG
1
2
3
4
5
6
7

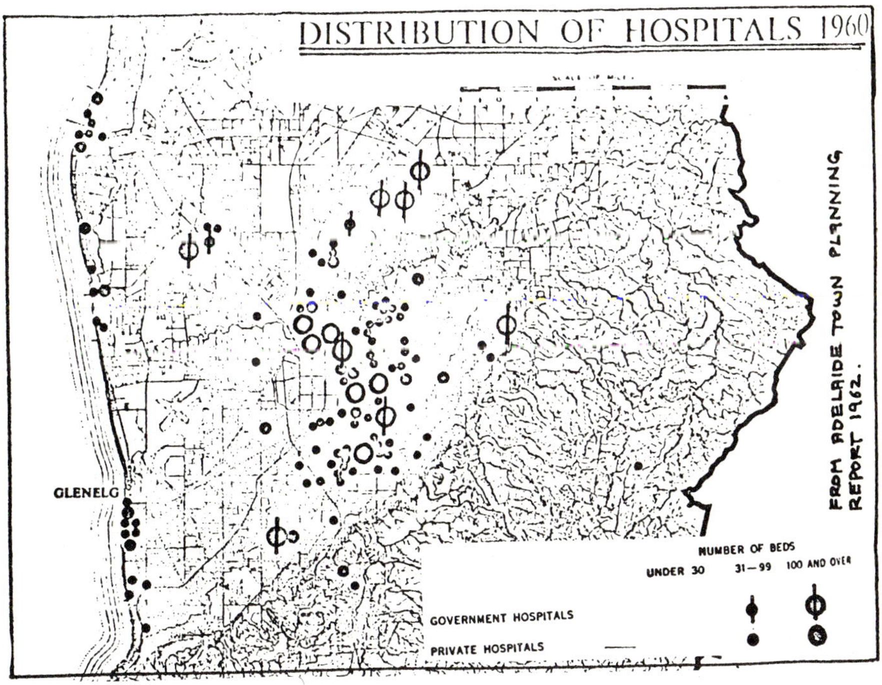
DISTRIBUTION OF HOSPITALS 1960
GLENELG
FROM ADELAIDE TOWN PLANNING
REPORT 1962.
NUMBER OF BEDS
UNDER 30
31—99
100 AND OVER
GOVERNMENT HOSPITALS
PRIVATE HOSPITALS

THE DORMITORY SUBURB

The decade of the 1960s has seen so great an expansion of the city of Adelaide that the projected map for 1992, drawn in 1960 by the Town Planning Committee, has nearly become fact. (See Map N). As Adelaide's outer suburbs grow further into the hills and along the coast; Glenelg becomes, by comparison, an inner suburb. The 1960 Function Plan proposes that Glenelg and a ring of development around Adelaide and at the port will become high density living areas. The latter half of the 1960s has seen the gradual fulfilment of that plan, but the beginning of the 1970s has seen its sudden dramatic mushrooming to reality.

Because of limited land, many modern flats are multi-storied and consequently give Glenelg a high residential density

Glenelg already supported a relatively high residential density in 1960. The Planning Committee felt that as few old houses had not been converted, and as Glenelg's area was limited, the suburb was unlikely to experience much growth over the next decade. The last open spaces were subdivided and some single storey blocks of flats were erected. (See photograph, p. 86.) Glenelg's prospects for business and commercial growth were improving but not particularly good. The suburb was experiencing a mild revival as an urban holiday centre, but other areas along the coast, such as Henley Beach, attracted equally large crowds on hot summer nights. In 1959, the Patawalonga was successfully re-styled into a large and well appointed boat harbour, at a cost of £120,000. In 1969, Glenelg built a new jetty after being 20 years without one. Even though the jetty cost $127,000, it does not compare with the size and magnificence of its predecessor.

MAP N.

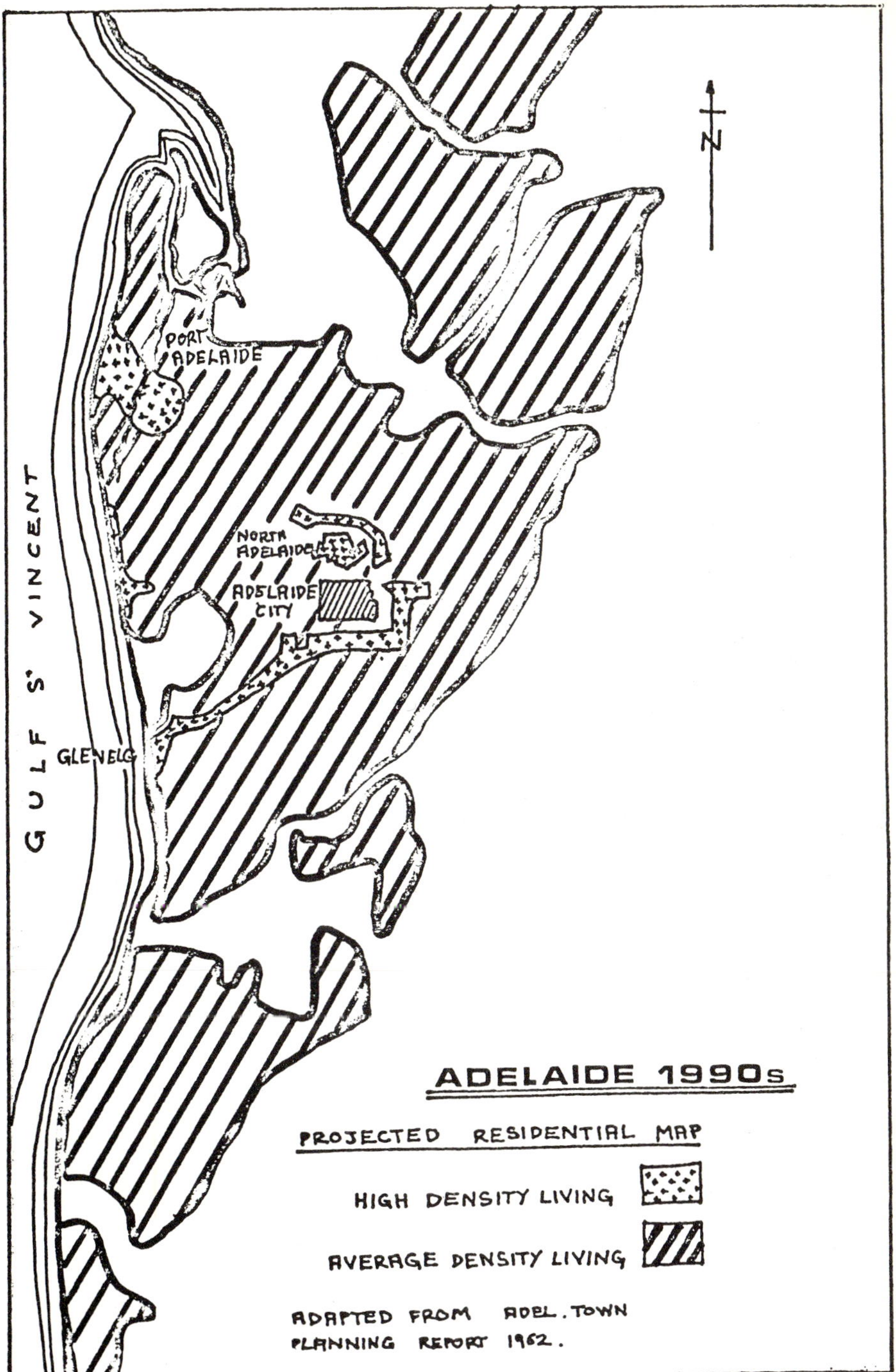
N
PORT ADELAIDE
NORTH ADELAIDE
ADELAIDE CITY
GLENELG
GULF S' VINCENT
ADELAIDE 1990s
PROJECTED RESIDENTIAL MAP
HIGH DENSITY LIVING
AVERAGE DENSITY LIVING
ADAPTED FROM ADEL. TOWN PLANNING REPORT 1962.

Examples of high density living, on a small scale and a large scale. Above, a block of flats and below, highrise living

(Author's photographs)

In the same year an extensive amusement park development scheme was finished, and along the coast to the north, a marineland was opened as a major tourist attraction. Efforts to bring business back to Glenelg resulted in carnivals, a jazz convention, and special incentives for married couples to return to Glenelg for a second honeymoon. The old yacht club house near the jetty was converted into an information centre and museum to promote tourism. Plans were submitted to borrow $105,000 to built an off-street parking station, but ratepayers rejected it. Glenelg, in the late 1960s, was undergoing a mild boom.

Quite suddenly, Glenelg was discovered. Although three and four storey blocks of flats were becoming quite common along Anzac Highway and in the residential areas of Adelaide, they had not, until the late 1960s, been extended into Glenelg. Glenelg was found to have unique possibilities for large-scale developments of high rise flats. Early in 1970, the ratepayers voted to continue the scheme of charging rates on the unimproved value of land.[4] This was an enormous incentive to high density building because nearer the heart of the city, the same blocks of flats would be charged on the improved value of the land and thus be vastly more expensive. Glenelg was clearly heading towards the fate of a dormitory suburb, which the subsequent rejection of this system of rates may have done little to prevent. It is particularly suited to flat and apartment living, for residents would be attracted by the pleasant surroundings of the sea and beach, combined with the extreme ease of access to the city. The motor car, which had sealed Glenelg's fate as a holiday resort, was now paradoxically building Glenelg's future as a high density dormitory suburb.

A suburban house in Glenelg which epitomises urban escapism. Note the gnome house, plaster flamingo and urn

(Author's photograph)

Across the road from Glenelg's oldest inn, St. Leonard's, rises the newest hotel

(Author's photographs)

The march of the home units brings St. Olives, a rest home, to the ground

By April of 1970, a building programme worth over four million dollars was in progress at Glenelg. Big local and interstate developers had made plans to invest many more millions in the near future. A Sydney based firm planned four blocks, two of 11 stories containing 37 units each and two of nine stories. The cheapest unit would cost $20,000 and the most expensive $45,000. Three such luxury apartments could cost as much as the entire jetty. Another development company was building a 14 storey circular motel on Anzac Highway, as well as a three storey block of flats. A third company was building a 13 storey block worth over half a million dollars. But the threat presented to Glenelg's identity by high-rise development may have been averted, for as of July 1972 the land rating system will be changed. Instead of being calculated on unimproved land value, rates will be calculated on rental value, which will mean a great increase in rates for highrise developments.

Less spectacular, but equally as important, the old houses that had been divided into flats some years before were being bulldozed to make room for home units. The same space that in the 1900s had housed one family, in the 1930s two families, would house six to eight families in the 1970s. Within one year in a small eastern section of Glenelg, Helmsdale, 14 of these home unit blocks were built, containing in all 63 units, worth nearly half a million dollars.[5] It seemed that Glenelg had no choice but to become a vast dormitory block for the citizens of Adelaide. Entertainments will no doubt develop to keep the migratory city happy while it is at home at night or during weekends. Perhaps the change in land rating system will provide some reprieve. By 1972, highrise blocks still

Above: Nearly all of Glenelg's old mansions stand doomed in the shadow of "For Sale" signs
Below: This high rise building will contain flats ranging in price from $35 to $75 a week

(Author's photographs)